# MznLnx

*Missing Links Exam Preps*

---

**Exam Prep for**

## Exploring Management: In Modules

### Schermerhorn, Jr., 1st Edition

The MznLnx Exam Prep is your link from the texbook and lecture to your exams.
The MznLnx Exam Preps are unauthorized and comprehensive reviews of your textbooks.

All material provided by MznLnx and Rico Publications (c) 2010
Textbook publishers and textbook authors do not particpate in or contribute to these reviews.

# MznLnx

## Rico Publications

*Exam Prep for Exploring Management: In Modules*
1st Edition
Schermerhorn, Jr.

*Publisher:* Raymond Houge
*Assistant Editor:* Michael Rouger
*Text and Cover Designer:* Lisa Buckner
*Marketing Manager:* Sara Swagger
*Project Manager, Editorial Production:* Jerry Emerson
*Art Director:* Vernon Lowerui

*Product Manager:* Dave Mason
*Editorial Assitant:* Rachel Guzmanji
*Pedagogy:* Debra Long
*Cover Image:* Jim Reed/Getty Images
*Text and Cover Printer:* City Printing, Inc.
*Compositor:* Media Mix, Inc.

(c) 2010 Rico Publications
ALL RIGHTS RESERVED. No part of this work covered by the copyright may be reproduced or used in any form or by an means--graphic, electronic, or mechanical, including photocopying, recording, taping, Web distribution, information storage, and retrieval systems, or in any other manner--without the written permission of the publisher.

Printed in the United States
ISBN:

For more information about our products, contact us at:
Dave.Mason@RicoPublications.com

For permission to use material from this text or product, submit a request online to:
Dave.Mason@RicoPublications.com

# Contents

**CHAPTER 1**
*Our New Workplace: This is no time for complacency* — 1

**CHAPTER 2**
*The Management Process: Everyone becomes a manager some day* — 6

**CHAPTER 3**
*Management Learning: Good things grow from strong foundations* — 10

**CHAPTER 4**
*Ethics and Ethical Behavior: Character doesn`t stay home when we go to work* — 15

**CHAPTER 5**
*Social Responsibility and Governance: Organizations have ethics too* — 19

**CHAPTER 6**
*Diversity and Global Cultures: There are new faces in the neighborhood* — 21

**CHAPTER 7**
*Globalization and International Business* — 24

**CHAPTER 8**
*Entrepreneurship and Small Businesses: It`s nice to be your own boss* — 31

**CHAPTER 9**
*Managers as Decision Makers: Decide first, then act* — 36

**CHAPTER 10**
*Plans and Planning Techniques: Goals and objectives get you there faster* — 40

**CHAPTER 11**
*Controls and Control Systems: Mat gets measured happens* — 44

**CHAPTER 12**
*Strategic Management: Insights and hard work deliver results* — 51

**CHAPTER 13**
*Organizational Structures: Its all about working together* — 56

**CHAPTER 14**
*Organizational Design and Culture: Adaptability and values set the tone* — 58

**CHAPTER 15**
*Human Resource Management: Nuturing turns potential into performance* — 60

**CHAPTER 16**
*Leadership: A leader lives in each of us* — 71

**CHAPTER 17**
*Communication: Listening can be the key to understanding* — 74

**CHAPTER 18**
*Individual Behavior: There`s beauty in individual differences* — 75

**CHAPTER 19**
*Motivation: Treat others as you would like to be treated* — 80

**CHAPTER 20**
*Motivational Dynamics: Money isn`t everything, the job counts too* — 84

# Contents (Cont.)

**CHAPTER 21**
*Teams and Teamwork: Two heads really can be better than one* — 88

**CHAPTER 22**
*Conflict and Negotiation: A smooth ride isn't always the best ride* — 91

**CHAPTER 23**
*Innovation and Change: Change can be your best friend* — 92

**ANSWER KEY** — 93

# TO THE STUDENT

### COMPREHENSIVE

The *MznLnx* Exam Prep series is designed to help you pass your exams. Editors at MznLnx review your textbooks and then prepare these practice exams to help you master the textbook material. Unlike study guides, workbooks, and practice tests provided by the texbook publisher and textbook authors, *MznLnx* gives you **all** of the material in each chapter in exam form, not just samples, so you can be sure to nail your exam.

### MECHANICAL

The MznLnx Exam Prep series creates exams that will help you learn the subject matter as well as test you on your understanding. Each question is designed to help you master the concept. Just working through the exams, you gain an understanding of the subject--its a simple mechanical process that produces success.

### INTEGRATED STUDY GUIDE AND REVIEW

MznLnx is not just a set of exams designed to test you, its also a comprehensive review of the subject content. Each exam question is also a review of the concept, making sure that you will get the answer correct without having to go to other sources of material. You learn as you go! Its the easiest way to pass an exam.

### HUMOR

Studying can be tedious and dry. MznLnx's instructional design includes moderate humor within the exam questions on occassion, to break the tedium and revitalize the brain

*Chapter 1. Our New Workplace: This is no time for complacency*  1

1. _____ is the set of processes, customs, policies, laws, and institutions affecting the way a corporation (or company) is directed, administered or controlled. _____ also includes the relationships among the many stakeholders involved and the goals for which the corporation is governed. The principal stakeholders are the shareholders/members, management, and the board of directors.
   a. Corporate governance
   b. Guarantee
   c. No-FEAR Act
   d. Flextime

2. _____ is a form of corporate self-regulation integrated into a business model. Ideally, _____ policy would function as a built-in, self-regulating mechanism whereby business would monitor and ensure their adherence to law, ethical standards, and international norms. Business would embrace responsibility for the impact of their activities on the environment, consumers, employees, communities, stakeholders and all other members of the public sphere.
   a. Corporate social responsibility
   b. 28-hour day
   c. 1990 Clean Air Act
   d. 33 Strategies of War

3. The _____ of 2002 (Pub.L. 107-204, 116 Stat. 745, enacted July 30, 2002), also known as the Public Company Accounting Reform and Investor Protection Act of 2002 and commonly called Sarbanes-Oxley, Sarbox or SOX, is a United States federal law enacted on July 30, 2002, as a reaction to a number of major corporate and accounting scandals including those affecting Enron, Tyco International, Adelphia, Peregrine Systems and WorldCom.
   a. Letter of credit
   b. Sarbanes-Oxley Act of 2002
   c. Fair Labor Standards Act
   d. Sarbanes-Oxley Act

4. The 'business case for _____', theorizes that in a global marketplace, a company that employs a diverse workforce (both men and women, people of many generations, people from ethnically and racially diverse backgrounds etc.) is better able to understand the demographics of the marketplace it serves and is thus better equipped to thrive in that marketplace than a company that has a more limited range of employee demographics.

   An additional corollary suggests that a company that supports the _____ of its workforce can also improve employee satisfaction, productivity and retention.

   a. Kanban
   b. Trademark
   c. Diversity
   d. Virtual team

## Chapter 1. Our New Workplace: This is no time for complacency

5. _____ in its literal sense is the process of transformation of local or regional phenomena into global ones. It can be described as a process by which the people of the world are unified into a single society and function together.

This process is a combination of economic, technological, sociocultural and political forces.

   a. Cost Management
   b. Collaborative Planning, Forecasting and Replenishment
   c. Histogram
   d. Globalization

6. _____ is a term that has gained widespread use in the recent years and although it means relocation of jobs from one geographical area to another, it has come to symbolize the migration or relocation of jobs to other countries.

In most situations jobs are moved from one location to another, or to multiple other locations, because of changes in one or many of the following: supply and demand for products and services, business conditions, labor markets, government policies, political reasons, competition, environmental conditions, local business costs, technological obsolescence, outsourcing, higher productivity, etc.

_____ usually leads to rise in unemployment often accompanied by a difficult transition to new jobs and new locations requiring new training and lowered living standards, although not for everyone.

   a. 1990 Clean Air Act
   b. 28-hour day
   c. Job Shadow
   d. Job migration

7. _____ is subcontracting a process, such as product design or manufacturing, to a third-party company. The decision to outsource is often made in the interest of lowering cost or making better use of time and energy costs, redirecting or conserving energy directed at the competencies of a particular business, or to make more efficient use of land, labor, capital, (information) technology and resources. _____ became part of the business lexicon during the 1980s.
   a. Operant conditioning
   b. Opinion leadership
   c. Unemployment insurance
   d. Outsourcing

8. The _____ is the labour pool in employment. It is generally used to describe those working for a single company or industry, but can also apply to a geographic region like a city, country, state, etc. The term generally excludes the employers or management, and implies those involved in manual labour.

a. Pink-collar worker
b. Division of labour
c. Work-life balance
d. Workforce

9. An _____ is a person who has possession of an enterprise and assumes significant accountability for the inherent risks and the outcome. It is an ambitious leader who combines land, labor, and capital to create and market new goods or services. The term is a loanword from French and was first defined by the Irish economist Richard Cantillon.

   a. Entrepreneur
   b. A Stake in the Outcome
   c. AAAI
   d. A4e

10. _____ is a mathematical science pertaining to the collection, analysis, interpretation or explanation, and presentation of data. It also provides tools for prediction and forecasting based on data. It is applicable to a wide variety of academic disciplines, from the natural and social sciences to the humanities, government and business.

    a. Simple moving average
    b. Statistics
    c. Location parameter
    d. Failure rate

11. In economics, the term _____ refers to situations where the advancement of a qualified person within the hierarchy of an organization is stopped at a lower level because of some form of discrimination, most commonly sexism or racism, but since the term was coined, '_____' has also come to describe the limited advancement of the deaf, blind, disabled, aged and sexual minorities. It is an unofficial, invisible barrier that prevents women and minorities from advancing in businesses.

This situation is referred to as a 'ceiling' as there is a limitation blocking upward advancement, and 'glass' (transparent) because the limitation is not immediately apparent and is normally an unwritten and unofficial policy. This invisible barrier continues to exist, even though there are no explicit obstacles keeping minorities from acquiring advanced job positions - there are no advertisements that specifically say 'no minorities hired at this establishment', nor are there any formal orders that say 'minorities are not qualified' - but they do lie beneath the surface.

   a. 1990 Clean Air Act
   b. 28-hour day
   c. 33 Strategies of War
   d. Glass ceiling

12. The term _____ collectively refers to all resources that determine the value and the competitiveness of an enterprise. As such, it includes as subsets the attributes that concur to building all financial statements as well as the balance sheet.
   a. A Stake in the Outcome
   b. AAAI
   c. A4e
   d. Intellectual capital

13. A _____ in today's workforce is an individual that is valued for their ability to interpret information within a specific subject area. They will often advance the overall understanding of that subject through focused analysis, design and/or development. They use research skills to define problems and to identify alternatives.
   a. Career development
   b. Customer satisfaction
   c. Business rule
   d. Knowledge worker

14. A _____ is a brief written statement of the purpose of a company or organization. Ideally, a _____ guides the actions of the organization, spells out its overall goal, provides a sense of direction, and guides decision making for all levels of management.

   _____s often contain the following:

   - Purpose and aim of the organization
   - The organization's primary stakeholders: clients, stockholders, etc.
   - Responsibilities of the organization toward these stakeholders
   - Products and services offered

   In developing a _____:

   - Encourage as much input as feasible from employees, volunteers, and other stakeholders
   - Publicize it broadly

   The _____ can be used to resolve differences between business stakeholders. Stakeholders include: employees including managers and executives, stockholders, board of directors, customers, suppliers, distributors, creditors, governments (local, state, federal, etc.), unions, competitors, NGO's, and the general public.

a. 28-hour day
b. 1990 Clean Air Act
c. 33 Strategies of War
d. Mission statement


15. The _____ is a concept from business management that was first described and popularized by Michael Porter in his 1985 best-seller, Competitive Advantage: Creating and Sustaining Superior Performance.

A _____ is a chain of activities. Products pass through all activities of the chain in order and at each activity the product gains some value. The chain of activities gives the products more added value than the sum of added values of all activities. It is important not to mix the concept of the _____ with the costs occurring throughout the activities.

a. Mass marketing
b. Market development
c. Customer relationship management
d. Value chain


16. In economics, business, retail, and accounting, a _____ is the value of money that has been used up to produce something, and hence is not available for use anymore. In economics, a _____ is an alternative that is given up as a result of a decision. In business, the _____ may be one of acquisition, in which case the amount of money expended to acquire it is counted as _____.
a. Cost overrun
b. Fixed costs
c. Cost allocation
d. Cost


17. _____ refers to metrics and measures of output from production processes, per unit of input. Labor _____, for example, is typically measured as a ratio of output per labor-hour, an input. _____ may be conceived of as a metrics of the technical or engineering efficiency of production.
a. Value engineering
b. Remanufacturing
c. Master production schedule
d. Productivity

## Chapter 2. The Management Process: Everyone becomes a manager some day

1. _____ is an advertisement in which a particular product specifically mentions a competitor by name for the express purpose of showing why the competitor is inferior to the product naming it.

This should not be confused with parody advertisements, where a fictional product is being advertised for the purpose of poking fun at the particular advertisement, nor should it be confused with the use of a coined brand name for the purpose of comparing the product without actually naming an actual competitor. ('Wikipedia tastes better and is less filling than the Encyclopedia Galactica.')

In the 1980s, during what has been referred to as the cola wars, soft-drink manufacturer Pepsi ran a series of advertisements where people, caught on hidden camera, in a blind taste test, chose Pepsi over rival Coca-Cola.

   a. 1990 Clean Air Act
   b. 28-hour day
   c. 33 Strategies of War
   d. Comparative advertising


2. _____ is a concept in ethics with several meanings. It is often used synonymously with such concepts as responsibility, answerability, enforcement, blameworthiness, liability and other terms associated with the expectation of account-giving. As an aspect of governance, it has been central to discussions related to problems in both the public and private (corporation) worlds.
   a. Usury
   b. A Stake in the Outcome
   c. A4e
   d. Accountability


3. A _____ is a body of elected or appointed members who jointly oversee the activities of a company or organization. The body sometimes has a different name, such as board of trustees, board of governors, board of managers, or executive board. It is often simply referred to as 'the board.'

A board's activities are determined by the powers, duties, and responsibilities delegated to it or conferred on it by an authority outside itself.

   a. Competition law
   b. Foreign Corrupt Practices Act
   c. Clean Water Act
   d. Board of Directors

## Chapter 2. The Management Process: Everyone becomes a manager some day

4. _____ is one of the managerial functions like planning, organizing, staffing and directing. It is an important function because it helps to check the errors and to take the corrective action so that deviation from standards are minimized and stated goals of the organization are achieved in desired manner. According to modern concepts, _____ is a foreseeing action whereas earlier concept of _____ was used only when errors were detected. _____ in management means setting standards, measuring actual performance and taking corrective action.
   a. Decision tree pruning
   b. Schedule of reinforcement
   c. Control
   d. Turnover

5. A _____ is a list of the general tasks and responsibilities of a position. Typically, it also includes to whom the position reports, specifications such as the qualifications needed by the person in the job, salary range for the position, etc. A _____ is usually developed by conducting a job analysis, which includes examining the tasks and sequences of tasks necessary to perform the job.
   a. Recruitment
   b. Recruitment advertising
   c. Recruitment Process Insourcing
   d. Job description

6. The _____ is a leadership theory in the field of organizational studies developed by Robert House in 1971 and revised in 1996. The theory that a leader's behavior is contingent to the satisfaction, motivation and performance of subordinates. The revised version also argues that the leader engage in behaviors that complement subordinate's abilities and compensate for deficiencies.
   a. Human relations
   b. Corporate Culture
   c. Sociotechnical systems
   d. Path-goal theory

7. The _____ is the theory that the mass-news media have a large influence on audiences by their choice of what stories to consider newsworthy and how much prominence and space to give them. _____'s main postulate is salience transfer. Salience transfer is the ability of the mass media to transfer issues of importance from their mass media agendas to public agendas.
   a. A Stake in the Outcome
   b. AAAI
   c. Agenda-setting theory
   d. A4e

## Chapter 2. The Management Process: Everyone becomes a manager some day

8. _____ , often measured as an _____ Quotient (EQ), is a term that describes the ability, capacity, skill or (in the case of the trait _____ model) a self-perceived ability, to identify, assess, and manage the emotions of one's self, of others, and of groups. Different models have been proposed for the definition of _____ and disagreement exists as to how the term should be used. Despite these disagreements, which are often highly technical, the ability _____ and trait _____ models (but not the mixed models) are enjoying considerable support in the literature and have successful applications in many different domains.
   a. AAAI
   b. A4e
   c. A Stake in the Outcome
   d. Emotional intelligence

9. _____ is purposeful and reflective judgment about what to believe or what to do in response to observations, experience, verbal or written expressions, or arguments. _____ might involve determining the meaning and significance of what is observed or expressed, or, concerning a given inference or argument, determining whether there is adequate justification to accept the conclusion as true. Hence, Fisher ' Scriven define _____ as 'Skilled, active, interpretation and evaluation of observations, communications, information, and argumentation.' Parker ' Moore define it more narrowly as the careful, deliberate determination of whether one should accept, reject, or suspend judgment about a claim and the degree of confidence with which one accepts or rejects it.
   a. Critical thinking
   b. Virtual team
   c. Risk management
   d. Kanban

10. _____ has been described as the 'process of social influence in which one person can enlist the aid and support of others in the accomplishment of a common task' . A definition more inclusive of followers comes from Alan Keith of Genentech who said '_____ is ultimately about creating a way for people to contribute to making something extraordinary happen.'

    _____ is one of the most salient aspects of the organizational context. However, defining _____ has been challenging.

   a. Situational leadership
   b. 28-hour day
   c. 1990 Clean Air Act
   d. Leadership

11. _____ is the 'lifelong, lifewide, voluntary, and self-motivated' pursuit of knowledge for either personal or professional reasons. As such, it not only enhances social inclusion, active citizenship and personal development, but also competitiveness and employability.

The term recognises that learning is not confined to childhood or the classroom, but takes place throughout life and in a range of situations.

a. 33 Strategies of War
b. 1990 Clean Air Act
c. 28-hour day
d. Lifelong learning

## Chapter 3. Management Learning: Good things grow from strong foundations

1. _____ is a commonly used, yet poorly defined concept in industrial and organizational psychology, the branch of psychology that deals with the workplace. It most commonly refers to whether a person performs their job well. Despite the confusion over how it should be exactly defined, performance is an extremely important criterion that relates to organizational outcomes and success.

   a. Job performance
   b. 33 Strategies of War
   c. 1990 Clean Air Act
   d. 28-hour day


2. _____ is a method by which the job performance of an employee is evaluated _____ is a part of career development.

   _____s are regular reviews of employee performance within organizations

   Generally, the aims of a _____ are to:

   - Give feedback on performance to employees.
   - Identify employee training needs.
   - Document criteria used to allocate organizational rewards.
   - Form a basis for personnel decisions: salary increases, promotions, disciplinary actions, etc.
   - Provide the opportunity for organizational diagnosis and development.
   - Facilitate communication between employee and administraton
   - Validate selection techniques and human resource policies to meet federal Equal Employment Opportunity requirements.

   A common approach to assessing performance is to use a numerical or scalar rating system whereby managers are asked to score an individual against a number of objectives/attributes. In some companies, employees receive assessments from their manager, peers, subordinates and customers while also performing a self assessment.

   a. Personnel management
   b. Performance appraisal
   c. Human resource management
   d. Progressive discipline


3. _____ is a theory of management that analyzes and synthesizes workflows, with the objective of improving labour productivity. The core ideas of the theory were developed by Frederick Winslow Taylor in the 1880s and 1890s, and were first published in his monographs, Shop Management and The Principles of _____ Taylor believed that decisions based upon tradition and rules of thumb should be replaced by precise procedures developed after careful study of an individual at work.

a. Capacity planning
b. Master production schedule
c. Value engineering
d. Scientific management


4. _____ describes how content an individual is with his or her job.

The happier people are within their job, the more satisfied they are said to be. _____ is not the same as motivation, although it is clearly linked.

a. Goal-setting theory
b. Job analysis
c. Job satisfaction
d. Human relations


5. The _____ is a form of reactivity whereby subjects improve an aspect of their behavior being experimentally measured simply in response to the fact that they are being studied, not in response to any particular experimental manipulation.

The term was coined in 1955 by Henry A. Landsberger when analyzing older experiments from 1924-1932 at the Hawthorne Works (outside Chicago.) Hawthorne Works had commissioned a study to see if its workers would become more productive in higher or lower levels of light.

a. Hawthorne effect
b. 1990 Clean Air Act
c. 33 Strategies of War
d. 28-hour day


6. _____ is a term that has been used in various psychology theories, often in slightly different ways (e.g., Goldstein, Maslow, Rogers.) The term was originally introduced by the organismic theorist Kurt Goldstein for the motive to realise all of one's potentialities. In his view, it is the master motive--indeed, the only real motive a person has, all others being merely manifestations of it.

a. 33 Strategies of War
b. Self-actualization
c. 1990 Clean Air Act
d. 28-hour day

7. In economics, the term _____ refers to situations where the advancement of a qualified person within the hierarchy of an organization is stopped at a lower level because of some form of discrimination, most commonly sexism or racism, but since the term was coined, '_____' has also come to describe the limited advancement of the deaf, blind, disabled, aged and sexual minorities. It is an unofficial, invisible barrier that prevents women and minorities from advancing in businesses.

This situation is referred to as a 'ceiling' as there is a limitation blocking upward advancement, and 'glass' (transparent) because the limitation is not immediately apparent and is normally an unwritten and unofficial policy. This invisible barrier continues to exist, even though there are no explicit obstacles keeping minorities from acquiring advanced job positions - there are no advertisements that specifically say 'no minorities hired at this establishment', nor are there any formal orders that say 'minorities are not qualified' - but they do lie beneath the surface.

   a. 33 Strategies of War
   b. 28-hour day
   c. 1990 Clean Air Act
   d. Glass ceiling


8. _____ and Theory Y are theories of human motivation created and developed by Douglas McGregor at the MIT Sloan School of Management in the 1960s that have been used in human resource management, organizational behavior, organizational communication and organizational development. They describe two very different attitudes toward workforce motivation. McGregor felt that companies followed either one or the other approach.

In _____, which many managers practice, management assumes employees are inherently lazy and will avoid work if they can. They inherently dislike work. Because of this, workers need to be closely supervised and comprehensive systems of controls developed.

   a. Job enrichment
   b. Theory X
   c. Cash cow
   d. Management team


9. Theory X and _____ are theories of human motivation created and developed by Douglas McGregor at the MIT Sloan School of Management in the 1960s that have been used in human resource management, organizational behavior, organizational communication and organizational development. They describe two very different attitudes toward workforce motivation. McGregor felt that companies followed either one or the other approach.

In _____, management assumes employees may be ambitious and self-motivated and exercise self-control. It is believed that employees enjoy their mental and physical work duties.

## Chapter 3. Management Learning: Good things grow from strong foundations

a. Theory Y
b. Contingency theory
c. Business Workflow Analysis
d. Design leadership

10. An _____ is a person who has possession of an enterprise and assumes significant accountability for the inherent risks and the outcome. It is an ambitious leader who combines land, labor, and capital to create and market new goods or services. The term is a loanword from French and was first defined by the Irish economist Richard Cantillon.
   a. Entrepreneur
   b. A4e
   c. A Stake in the Outcome
   d. AAAI

11. _____ refers to metrics and measures of output from production processes, per unit of input. Labor _____, for example, is typically measured as a ratio of output per labor-hour, an input. _____ may be conceived of as a metrics of the technical or engineering efficiency of production.
   a. Remanufacturing
   b. Master production schedule
   c. Value engineering
   d. Productivity

12. In management science, operations research and organizational development (OD), human organizations are viewed as systems (conceptual systems) of interacting components such as _____ or system aggregates, which are carriers of numerous complex processes and organizational structures. Organizational development theorist Peter Senge developed the notion of organizations as systems in his book The Fifth Discipline.

Systems thinking is a style of thinking/reasoning and problem solving.

   a. Subsystems
   b. 28-hour day
   c. 1990 Clean Air Act
   d. Systems thinking

13. A _____ is the term given to a company that facilitates the learning of its members and continuously transforms itself. _____s develop as a result of the pressures facing modern organizations and enables them to remain competitive in the business environment. A _____ has five main features; systems thinking, personal mastery, mental models, shared vision and team learning.

a. Learning organization
b. Hoshin Kanri
c. Quality function deployment
d. 1990 Clean Air Act

## Chapter 4. Ethics and Ethical Behavior: Character doesn't stay home when we go to work

1. _____ is the value of objects, both physical objects and abstract objects, not as ends-in-themselves but a means of achieving something else. It is often contrasted with items of intrinsic value.

It is studied in the field of value theory.

   a. A4e
   b. AAAI
   c. A Stake in the Outcome
   d. Instrumental value


2. A _____ occurs when an individual or organization (such as a policeman, lawyer, insurance adjuster, politician, engineer, executive, director of a corporation, medical research scientist, physician, writer, editor, or any other entrusted individual or organization) has an interest that might compromise their actions. The presence of a _____ is independent from the execution of impropriety.

In the legal profession, the duty of loyalty owed to a client prohibits an attorney (or a law firm) from representing any other party with interests adverse to those of a current client.

   a. Conflict of interest
   b. Global Corruption Report
   c. 1990 Clean Air Act
   d. 28-hour day


3. An _____ is a situation that will often involve an apparent conflict between moral imperatives, in which to obey one would result in transgressing another. This is also called an ethical paradox since in moral philosophy, paradox plays a central role in ethics debates. For instance, an ethical admonition to 'love thy neighbour as thy self' is not always just in contrast with, but sometimes in contradiction to an armed neighbour actively trying to kill you: if he or she succeeds, you will not be able to love him or her.
   a. AAAI
   b. A4e
   c. Ethical dilemma
   d. A Stake in the Outcome


4. _____ is unwelcome harassment of a sexual nature, or based upon the receiving party's sex or gender. In some contexts or circumstances, _____ may be illegal. It includes a range of behavior from seemingly mild transgressions and annoyances to actual sexual abuse or sexual assault.

## Chapter 4. Ethics and Ethical Behavior: Character doesn`t stay home when we go to work

   a. Sexual harassment
   b. 28-hour day
   c. Hypernorms
   d. 1990 Clean Air Act

5. In economics, business, retail, and accounting, a _____ is the value of money that has been used up to produce something, and hence is not available for use anymore. In economics, a _____ is an alternative that is given up as a result of a decision. In business, the _____ may be one of acquisition, in which case the amount of money expended to acquire it is counted as _____.
   a. Cost
   b. Fixed costs
   c. Cost allocation
   d. Cost overrun

6. _____ is a commonly used, yet poorly defined concept in industrial and organizational psychology, the branch of psychology that deals with the workplace. It most commonly refers to whether a person performs their job well. Despite the confusion over how it should be exactly defined, performance is an extremely important criterion that relates to organizational outcomes and success.

   a. 28-hour day
   b. 1990 Clean Air Act
   c. Job performance
   d. 33 Strategies of War

7. _____ is a method by which the job performance of an employee is evaluated _____ is a part of career development.

_____s are regular reviews of employee performance within organizations

*Chapter 4. Ethics and Ethical Behavior: Character doesn't stay home when we go to work*

Generally, the aims of a _____ are to:

- Give feedback on performance to employees.
- Identify employee training needs.
- Document criteria used to allocate organizational rewards.
- Form a basis for personnel decisions: salary increases, promotions, disciplinary actions, etc.
- Provide the opportunity for organizational diagnosis and development.
- Facilitate communication between employee and administraton
- Validate selection techniques and human resource policies to meet federal Equal Employment Opportunity requirements.

A common approach to assessing performance is to use a numerical or scalar rating system whereby managers are asked to score an individual against a number of objectives/attributes. In some companies, employees receive assessments from their manager, peers, subordinates and customers while also performing a self assessment.

a. Performance appraisal
b. Progressive discipline
c. Personnel management
d. Human resource management


8. _____ describes how content an individual is with his or her job.

The happier people are within their job, the more satisfied they are said to be. _____ is not the same as motivation, although it is clearly linked.

a. Goal-setting theory
b. Job satisfaction
c. Human relations
d. Job analysis


9. _____ according to Onuoha (2007) is the practice of starting new organizations or revitalizing mature organizations, particularly new businesses generally in response to identified opportunities. _____ is often a difficult undertaking, as a vast majority of new businesses fail. Entrepreneurial activities are substantially different depending on the type of organization that is being started.
a. AAAI
b. A4e
c. A Stake in the Outcome
d. Entrepreneurship

## Chapter 4. Ethics and Ethical Behavior: Character doesn't stay home when we go to work

10. A _____ is a person who alleges misconduct. More complex definitions may be used, but the issue is that the _____ usually faces reprisal. The misconduct may be classified in many ways; for example, a violation of a law, rule, regulation and/or a direct threat to public interest, such as fraud, health/safety violations, and corruption.

    a. 28-hour day
    b. 1990 Clean Air Act
    c. 33 Strategies of War
    d. Whistleblower

11. _____ is a concept in ethics with several meanings. It is often used synonymously with such concepts as responsibility, answerability, enforcement, blameworthiness, liability and other terms associated with the expectation of account-giving. As an aspect of governance, it has been central to discussions related to problems in both the public and private (corporation) worlds.

    a. Usury
    b. Accountability
    c. A4e
    d. A Stake in the Outcome

12. _____ of the learning curve effect and the closely related experience curve effect express the relationship between equations for experience and efficiency or between efficiency gains and investment in the effort. The experience of 'learning curves' was first observed by the 19th Century German psychologist Hermann Ebbinghaus according to the difficulty of memorizing varying numbers of verbal stimuli, and subsequent learning about the complex processes of learning are discussed in the

The rule used for representing the learning curve effect states that the more times a task has been performed, the less time will be required on each subsequent iteration.

    a. Distribution
    b. Spatial Decision Support Systems
    c. Point biserial correlation coefficient
    d. Models

## Chapter 5. Social Responsibility and Governance: Organizations have ethics too

1. _____ is a form of corporate self-regulation integrated into a business model. Ideally, _____ policy would function as a built-in, self-regulating mechanism whereby business would monitor and ensure their adherence to law, ethical standards, and international norms. Business would embrace responsibility for the impact of their activities on the environment, consumers, employees, communities, stakeholders and all other members of the public sphere.
   a. Corporate social responsibility
   b. 1990 Clean Air Act
   c. 33 Strategies of War
   d. 28-hour day

2. The general definition of an _____ is an evaluation of a person, organization, system, process, project or product. _____s are performed to ascertain the validity and reliability of information; also to provide an assessment of a system's internal control. The goal of an _____ is to express an opinion on the person / organization/system (etc) in question, under evaluation based on work done on a test basis.
   a. Audit
   b. Internal control
   c. Audit committee
   d. A Stake in the Outcome

3. A _____ or a vicious circle (sometimes referred to as 'cycle' instead of 'circle') is a complex of events that reinforces itself through a feedback loop. A _____ has favorable results, and a vicious circle has detrimental results. A _____ can transform into a vicious circle if eventual negative feedback is ignored.
   a. Defined benefit pension plan
   b. Power
   c. Fixed asset turnover
   d. Virtuous circle

4. _____ is the set of processes, customs, policies, laws, and institutions affecting the way a corporation (or company) is directed, administered or controlled. _____ also includes the relationships among the many stakeholders involved and the goals for which the corporation is governed. The principal stakeholders are the shareholders/members, management, and the board of directors.
   a. Guarantee
   b. No-FEAR Act
   c. Flextime
   d. Corporate governance

5. The _____ of 2002 (Pub.L. 107-204, 116 Stat. 745, enacted July 30, 2002), also known as the Public Company Accounting Reform and Investor Protection Act of 2002 and commonly called Sarbanes-Oxley, Sarbox or SOX, is a United States federal law enacted on July 30, 2002, as a reaction to a number of major corporate and accounting scandals including those affecting Enron, Tyco International, Adelphia, Peregrine Systems and WorldCom.

a. Fair Labor Standards Act
b. Letter of credit
c. Sarbanes-Oxley Act of 2002
d. Sarbanes-Oxley Act


6. _____ is a concept in ethics with several meanings. It is often used synonymously with such concepts as responsibility, answerability, enforcement, blameworthiness, liability and other terms associated with the expectation of account-giving. As an aspect of governance, it has been central to discussions related to problems in both the public and private (corporation) worlds.
a. A4e
b. Accountability
c. Usury
d. A Stake in the Outcome

## Chapter 6. Diversity and Global Cultures: There are new faces in the neighborhood

1. The 'business case for _____', theorizes that in a global marketplace, a company that employs a diverse workforce (both men and women, people of many generations, people from ethnically and racially diverse backgrounds etc.) is better able to understand the demographics of the marketplace it serves and is thus better equipped to thrive in that marketplace than a company that has a more limited range of employee demographics.

   An additional corollary suggests that a company that supports the _____ of its workforce can also improve employee satisfaction, productivity and retention.

   a. Virtual team
   b. Trademark
   c. Kanban
   d. Diversity


2. In sociology, anthropology and cultural studies, a _____ is a group of people with a culture (whether distinct or hidden) which differentiates them from the larger culture to which they belong. If a particular _____ is characterized by a systematic opposition to the dominant culture, it may be described as a counterculture.

   As early as 1950, David Riesman distinguished between a majority, 'which passively accepted commercially provided styles and meanings, and a '_____' which actively sought a minority style ...

   a. 28-hour day
   b. Subculture
   c. 1990 Clean Air Act
   d. 33 Strategies of War


3. In economics, the term _____ refers to situations where the advancement of a qualified person within the hierarchy of an organization is stopped at a lower level because of some form of discrimination, most commonly sexism or racism, but since the term was coined, '_____' has also come to describe the limited advancement of the deaf, blind, disabled, aged and sexual minorities. It is an unofficial, invisible barrier that prevents women and minorities from advancing in businesses.

   This situation is referred to as a 'ceiling' as there is a limitation blocking upward advancement, and 'glass' (transparent) because the limitation is not immediately apparent and is normally an unwritten and unofficial policy. This invisible barrier continues to exist, even though there are no explicit obstacles keeping minorities from acquiring advanced job positions - there are no advertisements that specifically say 'no minorities hired at this establishment', nor are there any formal orders that say 'minorities are not qualified' - but they do lie beneath the surface.

**22** *Chapter 6. Diversity and Global Cultures: There are new faces in the neighborhood*

a. Glass ceiling
b. 1990 Clean Air Act
c. 33 Strategies of War
d. 28-hour day

4. An _____ is a person who has possession of an enterprise and assumes significant accountability for the inherent risks and the outcome. It is an ambitious leader who combines land, labor, and capital to create and market new goods or services. The term is a loanword from French and was first defined by the Irish economist Richard Cantillon.
a. Entrepreneur
b. A4e
c. A Stake in the Outcome
d. AAAI

5. The _____ is a leadership theory in the field of organizational studies developed by Robert House in 1971 and revised in 1996. The theory that a leader's behavior is contingent to the satisfaction, motivation and performance of subordinates. The revised version also argues that the leader engage in behaviors that complement subordinate's abilities and compensate for deficiencies.
a. Sociotechnical systems
b. Corporate Culture
c. Human relations
d. Path-goal theory

6. _____, cultural quotient or CQ, is a theory within management and organisational psychology, positing that understanding the impact of an individual's cultural background on their behaviour is essential for effective business, and measuring an individual's ability to engage successfully in any environment or social setting. First described by Christopher Earley and Soon Ang in _____: Individual Interactions Across Cultures. The book was published in 2003 by Stanford University.
a. Cultural intelligence
b. Time to market
c. Sole proprietorship
d. Free cash flow

7. The term _____ was introduced by anthropologist Edward T. Hall in 1966 to describe set measurable distances between people as they interact. The effects of _____, according to Hall, can be summarized by the following loose rule:

*Chapter 6. Diversity and Global Cultures: There are new faces in the neighborhood*     23

According to Jonathon Tabor distance-spacing theories based on the early animal-like human of German zoologist Heini Hediger, as found in his 1955 book Studies of the Behavior of Captive Animals in Zoos and Circuses. Hediger, in animals, had distinguished between flight distance , critical distance (attack boundary), personal distance (distance separating members of non-contact species, as a pair of swans), and social distance (intraspecies communication distance.)

a. 28-hour day
b. 33 Strategies of War
c. 1990 Clean Air Act
d. Proxemics


8. _____ refers to the movement of cash into or out of a business or financial product. It is usually measured during a specified, finite period of time. Measurement of _____ can be used

- to determine a project's rate of return or value. The time of _____s into and out of projects are used as inputs in financial models such as internal rate of return, and net present value.
- to determine problems with a business's liquidity. Being profitable does not necessarily mean being liquid. A company can fail because of a shortage of cash, even while profitable.
- as an alternate measure of a business's profits when it is believed that accrual accounting concepts do not represent economic realities. For example, a company may be notionally profitable but generating little operational cash (as may be the case for a company that barters its products rather than selling for cash.) In such a case, the company may be deriving additional operating cash by issuing shares evaluating default risk, re-investment requirements, etc.

_____ is a generic term used differently depending on the context. It may be defined by users for their own purposes.

a. Sweat equity
b. Gross profit
c. Cash flow
d. Gross profit margin

## Chapter 7. Globalization and International Business

1. _____ is the branch of economics that studies the dynamics of exchange rates, foreign investment, and how these affect international trade. It also studies international projects, international investments and capital flows, and trade deficits. It includes the study of futures, options and currency swaps.
   a. AAAI
   b. International finance
   c. A Stake in the Outcome
   d. A4e

2. _____ is a term used to describe practice of sourcing from the global market for goods and services across geopolitical boundaries. _____ often aims to exploit global efficiencies in the delivery of a product or service. These efficiencies include low cost skilled labor, low cost raw material and other economic factors like tax breaks and low trade tariffs.
   a. Purchase requisition
   b. 1990 Clean Air Act
   c. Global sourcing
   d. Purchasing process

3. _____ in its literal sense is the process of transformation of local or regional phenomena into global ones. It can be described as a process by which the people of the world are unified into a single society and function together.

   This process is a combination of economic, technological, sociocultural and political forces.

   a. Cost Management
   b. Globalization
   c. Histogram
   d. Collaborative Planning, Forecasting and Replenishment

## Chapter 7. Globalization and International Business

4. In business, the term word _____ refers to a number of procurement practices, aimed at finding, evaluating and engaging suppliers of goods and services:

- Global _____, a procurement strategy aimed at exploiting global efficiencies in production
- Strategic _____, a component of supply chain management, for improving and re-evaluating purchasing activities
- _____, the identification of job candidates through proactive recruiting technique
- Co-_____, a type of auditing service
- Low-cost country _____, a procurement strategy for acquiring materials from countries with lower labour and production costs in order to cut operating expenses
- Corporate _____, a supply chain, purchasing/procurement, and inventory function
- Second-tier _____, a practice of rewarding suppliers for attempting to achieve minority-owned business spending goals of their customer
- Netsourcing, a practice of utilizing an established group of businesses, individuals, or hardware ' software applications to streamline or initiate procurement practices by tapping in to and working through a third party provider
- Inverted _____, a price volatility reduction strategy usually conducted by procurement or supply-chain person by which the value of an organization's waste-stream is maximized by actively seeking out the highest price possible from a range of potential buyers exploiting price trends and other market factors
- Multisourcing, a strategy that treats a given function, such as IT, as a portfolio of activities, some of which should be outsourced and others of which should be performed by internal staff.
- Crowdsourcing, using an undefined, generally large group of people or community in the form of an open call to perform a task

In journalism, it can also refer to:

- Journalism _____, the practice of identifying a person or publication that gives information
- Single _____, the reuse of content in publishing

In computing, it can refer to:

- Open-_____, the act of releasing previously proprietary software under an open source/free software license
- Power _____ equipment, network devices that will provide power in a Power over Ethernet (PoE) setup


a. Reinforcement
b. Continuous
c. Cost Management
d. Sourcing


5. _____ is exchange of capital, goods, and services across international borders or territories. In most countries, it represents a significant share of gross domestic product (GDP.) While _____ has been present throughout much of history , its economic, social, and political importance has been on the rise in recent centuries.

a. International trade
b. A Stake in the Outcome
c. AAAI
d. A4e

6. _____ refers to the methods of practicing and using another person's business philosophy. The franchisor grants the independent operator the right to distribute its products, techniques, and trademarks for a percentage of gross monthly sales and a royalty fee. Various tangibles and intangibles such as national or international advertising, training, and other support services are commonly made available by the franchisor.

a. 28-hour day
b. Franchising
c. ServiceMaster
d. 1990 Clean Air Act

7. A _____ is an entity formed between two or more parties to undertake economic activity together. The parties agree to create a new entity by both contributing equity, and they then share in the revenues, expenses, and control of the enterprise. The venture can be for one specific project only, or a continuing business relationship such as the Fuji Xerox _____.

a. Joint venture
b. Patent
c. Meritor Savings Bank v. Vinson
d. Civil Rights Act of 1991

8. A _____ is a formal relationship between two or more parties to pursue a set of agreed upon goals or to meet a critical business need while remaining independent organizations.

Partners may provide the _____ with resources such as products, distribution channels, manufacturing capability, project funding, capital equipment, knowledge, expertise, or intellectual property. The alliance is a cooperation or collaboration which aims for a synergy where each partner hopes that the benefits from the alliance will be greater than those from individual efforts.

a. Farmshoring
b. Process automation
c. Golden parachute
d. Strategic alliance

## Chapter 7. Globalization and International Business

9. An _____ is a person who has possession of an enterprise and assumes significant accountability for the inherent risks and the outcome. It is an ambitious leader who combines land, labor, and capital to create and market new goods or services. The term is a loanword from French and was first defined by the Irish economist Richard Cantillon.

   a. AAAI
   b. A4e
   c. A Stake in the Outcome
   d. Entrepreneur

10. The _____ is an international organization designed by its founders to supervise and liberalize international trade. The organization officially commenced on 1 January 1995, under the Marrakesh Agreement, succeeding the 1947 General Agreement on Tariffs and Trade (GATT.)

    The _____ deals with regulation of trade between participating countries; it provides a framework for negotiating and formalising trade agreements, and a dispute resolution process aimed at enforcing participants' adherence to _____ agreements which are signed by representatives of member governments and ratified by their parliaments.

    a. National Institute for Occupational Safety and Health
    b. 1990 Clean Air Act
    c. World Trade Organization
    d. Network planning and design

11. A _____ or transnational corporation is a corporation or enterprise that manages production or delivers services in more than one country. It can also be referred to as an international corporation.

    The first modern _____ is generally thought to be the Dutch East India Company, established in 1602.

    a. Small and medium enterprises
    b. Command center
    c. Financial Accounting Standards Board
    d. Multinational corporation

## Chapter 7. Globalization and International Business

12. _____ is a form of risk that arises from the change in price of one currency against another. Whenever investors or companies have assets or business operations across national borders, they face _____ if their positions are not hedged.

- Transaction risk is the risk that exchange rates will change unfavourably over time. It can be hedged against using forward currency contracts;
- Translation risk is an accounting risk, proportional to the amount of assets held in foreign currencies. Changes in the exchange rate over time will render a report inaccurate, and so assets are usually balanced by borrowings in that currency.

The exchange risk associated with a foreign denominated instrument is a key element in foreign investment. This risk flows from differential monetary policy and growth in real productivity, which results in differential inflation rates.

a. 1990 Clean Air Act
b. Currency risk
c. Taleb distribution
d. Market risk

13. _____ is a pattern of resource use that aims to meet human needs while preserving the environment so that these needs can be met not only in the present, but also for future generations. The term was used by the Brundtland Commission which coined what has become the most often-quoted definition of _____ as development that 'meets the needs of the present without compromising the ability of future generations to meet their own needs.'

_____ ties together concern for the carrying capacity of natural systems with the social challenges facing humanity. As early as the 1970s 'sustainability' was employed to describe an economy 'in equilibrium with basic ecological support systems.' Ecologists have pointed to the 'limits of growth' and presented the alternative of a 'steady state economy' in order to address environmental concerns.

a. Sustainability reporting
b. Sustainable business
c. Global Reporting Initiative
d. Sustainable development

14. A _____ is a working environment with conditions that are considered by many people of industrialized nations to be difficult or dangerous, usually where the workers have few opportunities to address their situation. This can include exposure to harmful materials, hazardous situations, extreme temperatures, or abuse from employers. _____ workers often work long hours for little pay, regardless of any laws mandating overtime pay or a minimum wage.

a. Complement
b. Continuous
c. Rate of return
d. Sweatshop

15. In decision theory and estimation theory, the _____ of an estimator, $\hat{\theta}$, of an unknown parameter of the distribution, θ, is the expected value of the loss function

$$R(\theta, \hat{\theta}) = \mathbb{E}_\theta L(\theta, \hat{\theta}) = \int L(\theta, \hat{\theta}) \, dP_\theta.$$

where $dP_\theta$ is a probability measure parametrized by θ.

- For a scalar parameter θ and a quadratic loss function,

$$L(\theta, \hat{\theta}) = (\theta - \hat{\theta})^2$$

the _____ function becomes the mean squared error of the estimate,

$$R(\theta, \hat{\theta}) = E_\theta (\theta - \hat{\theta})^2$$

- In density estimation, the unknown parameter is probability density itself. The loss function is typically chosen to be a norm in an appropriate function space. For example, for $L^2$ norm,

$$L(f, \hat{f}) = \|f - \hat{f}\|_2^2$$

the _____ function becomes the mean integrated squared error

$$R(f, \hat{f}) = E\|f - \hat{f}\|^2$$

a. Linear model
b. Financial modeling
c. Risk aversion
d. Risk

## Chapter 7. Globalization and International Business

16. An _____ is a person temporarily or permanently residing in a country and culture other than that of the person's upbringing or legal residence. The word comes from the Latin ex and patria (country, fatherland.)

The term is sometimes used in the context of Westerners living in non-Western countries, although it is also used to describe Westerners living in other Western countries, such as Americans living in the United Kingdom, or Britons living in Spain.

a. A4e
b. AAAI
c. Expatriate
d. A Stake in the Outcome

## Chapter 8. Entrepreneurship and Small Businesses: It`s nice to be your own boss

1. An _____ is a person who has possession of an enterprise and assumes significant accountability for the inherent risks and the outcome. It is an ambitious leader who combines land, labor, and capital to create and market new goods or services. The term is a loanword from French and was first defined by the Irish economist Richard Cantillon.
   a. A Stake in the Outcome
   b. AAAI
   c. A4e
   d. Entrepreneur

2. _____ according to Onuoha (2007) is the practice of starting new organizations or revitalizing mature organizations, particularly new businesses generally in response to identified opportunities. _____ is often a difficult undertaking, as a vast majority of new businesses fail. Entrepreneurial activities are substantially different depending on the type of organization that is being started.
   a. A4e
   b. A Stake in the Outcome
   c. AAAI
   d. Entrepreneurship

3. _____ is the advantage gained by the initial occupant of a market segment. This advantage may stem from the fact that the first entrant can gain control of resources that followers may not be able to match. Sometimes the first mover is not able to capitalise on its advantage, leaving the opportunity for another firm to gain second-mover advantage.
   a. Horizontal integration
   b. Customer retention
   c. Business ecosystem
   d. First-mover advantage

4. A _____ is a business that is privately owned and operated, with a small number of employees and relatively low volume of sales. The legal definition of 'small' often varies by country and industry, but is generally under 100 employees in the United States and under 50 employees in the European Union. In comparison, the definition of mid-sized business by the number of employees is generally under 500 in the U.S. and 250 for the European Union.
   a. Small business
   b. Pre-determined overhead rate
   c. Golden Boot Compensation
   d. Critical Success Factor

5. A _____ is a formal statement of a set of business goals, the reasons why they are believed attainable, and the plan for reaching those goals. It may also contain background information about the organization or team attempting to reach those goals.

The business goals may be defined for for-profit or for non-profit organizations.

a. Distributed management
b. Crisis management
c. Time management
d. Business plan

6. A _____ also known as a sole trader, or simply proprietorship is a type of business entity which there is only one owner and he has the final word taking all desicions by himself. All debts of the business are debts of the owner and must pay from his personal possessions. This means that the owner has unlimited liabilty.
   a. Golden hello
   b. Foreign ownership
   c. Business rule
   d. Sole proprietorship

7. In the commercial and legal parlance of most countries, a _____ or simply a partnership, refers to an association of persons or an unincorporated company with the following major features:

   - Created by agreement, proof of existence and estoppel.
   - Formed by two or more persons
   - The owners are all personally liable for any legal actions and debts the company may face

   It is a partnership in which partners share equally in both responsibility and liability.

   Partnerships have certain default characteristics relating to both the relationship between the individual partners and (b) the relationship between the partnership and the outside world. The former can generally be overridden by agreement between the partners, whereas the latter generally cannot be.

   The assets of the business are owned on behalf of the other partners, and they are each personally liable, jointly and severally, for business debts, taxes or tortious liability.

   a. Prospero Business Suite
   b. National Center for Trauma-Informed Care
   c. Business Roundtable
   d. General partnership

8. _____ is a concept whereby a person's financial liability is limited to a fixed sum, most commonly the value of a person's investment in a company or partnership with _____. In other words, if a company with _____ is sued, then the plaintiffs are suing the company, not its owners or investors. A shareholder in a limited company is not personally liable for any of the debts of the company, other than for the value of his investment in that company.

a. Partnership
b. Toxic Substances Control Act
c. Limited liability
d. Privity

9. A limited liability company in the law of the vast majority of United States jurisdictions is a legal form of business company that provides limited liability to its owners. Often incorrectly called a '_____' (instead of company), it is a hybrid business entity having certain characteristics of both a corporation and a partnership or sole proprietorship (depending on how many owners there are.) The primary characteristic an _____ shares with a corporation is limited liability, and the primary characteristic it shares with a partnership is the availability of pass-through income taxation.

   a. Growth capital
   b. Limited liability corporation
   c. Seed round
   d. Management buyout

10. In the United Kingdom _____s are governed by the _____s Act 2000 (in England and Wales and Scotland) and the _____s Act (Northern Ireland) 2002 in Northern Ireland. A UK _____ is a Corporate body - that is to say, it has a continuing legal existence independent of its Members, as compared to a Partnership which may (in England and Wales they do not) have a legal existence dependent upon its Membership.

A UK _____'s members have a collective ('Joint') responsibility, to the extent that they may agree in an '_____ agreement', but no individual ('several') responsibility for each other's actions.

   a. Small and medium enterprises
   b. Limited liability partnership
   c. Chief risk officer
   d. Compensation methods

11. A _____ is a type of business entity in which partners (owners) share with each other the profits or losses of the business. _____s are often favored over corporations for taxation purposes, as the _____ structure does not generally incur a tax on profits before it is distributed to the partners (i.e. there is no dividend tax levied.) However, depending on the _____ structure and the jurisdiction in which it operates, owners of a _____ may be exposed to greater personal liability than they would as shareholders of a corporation.

   a. Federal Employers Liability Act
   b. Mediation
   c. Due process
   d. Partnership

## Chapter 8. Entrepreneurship and Small Businesses: It's nice to be your own boss

12. An _____ or angel is an affluent individual who provides capital for a business start-up, usually in exchange for convertible debt or ownership equity. A small but increasing number of _____s organize themselves into angel groups or angel networks to share research and pool their investment capital.

Angels typically invest their own funds, unlike venture capitalists, who manage the pooled money of others in a professionally-managed fund.

   a. A Stake in the Outcome
   b. A4e
   c. AAAI
   d. Angel investor


13. _____ , also referred to simply as a 'public offering' or 'flotation,' is when a company issues common stock or shares to the public for the first time. They are often issued by smaller, younger companies seeking capital to expand, but can also be done by large privately-owned companies looking to become publicly traded.

In an _____ the issuer may obtain the assistance of an underwriting firm, which helps it determine what type of security to issue (common or preferred), best offering price and time to bring it to market.

   a. Initial public offering
   b. Outsourcing
   c. Unemployment insurance
   d. Occupational Safety and Health Administration


14. A _____ is a person or investment firm that makes venture investments, and these _____s are expected to bring managerial and technical expertise as well as capital to their investments. A venture capital fund refers to a pooled investment vehicle that primarily invests the financial capital of third-party investors in enterprises that are too risky for the standard capital markets or bank loans.

Venture capital is also associated with job creation, the knowledge economy and used as a proxy measure of innovation within an economic sector or geography.

   a. Limited partners
   b. Venture capitalist
   c. Limited liability corporation
   d. Private equity


15. An _____ is any party that makes an investment.

The term has taken on a specific meaning in finance to describe the particular types of people and companies that regularly purchase equity or debt securities for financial gain in exchange for funding an expanding company. Less frequently, the term is applied to parties who purchase real estate, currency, commodity derivatives, personal property, or other assets.

a. A4e
b. A Stake in the Outcome
c. Investor
d. AAAI

# Chapter 9. Managers as Decision Makers: Decide first, then act

1. _____ is a concept in ethics with several meanings. It is often used synonymously with such concepts as responsibility, answerability, enforcement, blameworthiness, liability and other terms associated with the expectation of account-giving. As an aspect of governance, it has been central to discussions related to problems in both the public and private (corporation) worlds.
   a. A Stake in the Outcome
   b. A4e
   c. Usury
   d. Accountability

2. In decision theory and estimation theory, the _____ of an estimator, $\hat{\theta}$, of an unknown parameter of the distribution, θ, is the expected value of the loss function

$$R(\theta, \hat{\theta}) = \mathbb{E}_\theta L(\theta, \hat{\theta}) = \int L(\theta, \hat{\theta})\, dP_\theta.$$

where $dP_\theta$ is a probability measure parametrized by θ.

- For a scalar parameter θ and a quadratic loss function,

$$L(\theta, \hat{\theta}) = (\theta - \hat{\theta})^2$$

  the _____ function becomes the mean squared error of the estimate,

$$R(\theta, \hat{\theta}) = \mathbb{E}_\theta (\theta - \hat{\theta})^2$$

- In density estimation, the unknown parameter is probability density itself. The loss function is typically chosen to be a norm in an appropriate function space. For example, for $L^2$ norm,

$$L(f, \hat{f}) = \|f - \hat{f}\|_2^2$$

  the _____ function becomes the mean integrated squared error

$$R(f, \hat{f}) = E\|f - \hat{f}\|^2$$

a. Linear model
b. Financial modeling
c. Risk
d. Risk aversion


3. _____ is a term that refers both to:

- a formal discipline used to help appraise, or assess, the case for a project or proposal, which itself is a process known as project appraisal; and
- an informal approach to making decisions of any kind.

Under both definitions the process involves, whether explicitly or implicitly, weighing the total expected costs against the total expected benefits of one or more actions in order to choose the best or most profitable option. The formal process is often referred to as either CBA (_____) or BCost-benefit analysis

A hallmark of CBA is that all benefits and all costs are expressed in money terms, and are adjusted for the time value of money, so that all flows of benefits and flows of project costs over time (which tend to occur at different points in time) are expressed on a common basis in terms of their 'present value.' Closely related, but slightly different, formal techniques include Cost-effectiveness analysis, Economic impact analysis, Fiscal impact analysis and Social Return on Investment(SROI) analysis. The latter builds upon the logic of _____, but differs in that it is explicitly designed to inform the practical decision-making of enterprise managers and investors focused on optimising their social and environmental impacts.

a. Decision engineering
b. Gittins index
c. Kepner-Tregoe
d. Cost-benefit analysis


4. Appraisal is the third and last stage in using formal decision methods. The objective of the appraisal stage is for the decision maker to develop insight into the decision and determine a clear course of action. Much of the insight developed in this stage results from exploring the implications of the formal _____ developed during the formulation stage (i.e., from mining the model.)
a. Nominal group technique
b. Decision Matrix
c. Kepner-Tregoe
d. Decision model

## Chapter 9. Managers as Decision Makers: Decide first, then act

5. _____ of the learning curve effect and the closely related experience curve effect express the relationship between equations for experience and efficiency or between efficiency gains and investment in the effort. The experience of 'learning curves' was first observed by the 19th Century German psychologist Hermann Ebbinghaus according to the difficulty of memorizing varying numbers of verbal stimuli, and subsequent learning about the complex processes of learning are discussed in the

The rule used for representing the learning curve effect states that the more times a task has been performed, the less time will be required on each subsequent iteration.

a. Spatial Decision Support Systems
b. Distribution
c. Point biserial correlation coefficient
d. Models

6. The _____ is a phenomenon (which can result in a cognitive bias) in which people base their prediction of the frequency of an event or the proportion within a population based on how easily an example can be brought to mind.

Simply stated, where an anecdote ('I know an American guy who...') is used to 'prove' an entire proposition or to support a bias, the _____ is in play.

In these instances the ease of imagining an example or the vividness and emotional impact of that example becomes more credible than actual statistical probability.

a. Availability heuristic
b. A Stake in the Outcome
c. AAAI
d. A4e

7. The _____ heuristic is a heuristic wherein people assume commonality between objects of similar appearance, or between an object and a group it appears to fit into. While often very useful in everyday life, it can also result in neglect of relevant base rates and other cognitive biases. The representative heuristic was first proposed by Amos Tversky and Daniel Kahneman.
   a. 28-hour day
   b. 1990 Clean Air Act
   c. Representativeness heuristic
   d. Representativeness

## Chapter 9. Managers as Decision Makers: Decide first, then act

8. The _____ is a heuristic wherein people assume commonality between objects of similar appearance, or between an object and a group it appears to fit into. While often very useful in everyday life, it can also result in neglect of relevant base rates and other errors. The representative heuristic was first proposed by Amos Tversky and Daniel Kahneman.
   a. 1990 Clean Air Act
   b. 28-hour day
   c. Representativeness
   d. Representativeness heuristic

9. _____ is an adjective for experience-based techniques that help in problem solving, learning and discovery. A _____ method is particularly used to rapidly come to a solution that is hoped to be close to the best possible answer, or 'optimal solution'. _____s are 'rules of thumb', educated guesses, intuitive judgments or simply common sense.
   a. Heuristic
   b. 28-hour day
   c. Representativeness
   d. 1990 Clean Air Act

10. _____ is decision making in groups consisting of multiple members/entities. The challenge of group decision is deciding what action a group should take. There are various systems designed to solve this problem.
    a. Control of Substances Hazardous to Health Regulations 2002
    b. Genbutsu
    c. Collaborative Planning, Forecasting and Replenishment
    d. Groups decision making

11. _____ can be regarded as an outcome of mental processes (cognitive process) leading to the selection of a course of action among several alternatives. Every _____ process produces a final choice. The output can be an action or an opinion of choice.
    a. 1990 Clean Air Act
    b. 33 Strategies of War
    c. Decision making
    d. 28-hour day

## Chapter 10. Plans and Planning Techniques: Goals and objectives get you there faster

1. A _____ is a list of the general tasks and responsibilities of a position. Typically, it also includes to whom the position reports, specifications such as the qualifications needed by the person in the job, salary range for the position, etc. A _____ is usually developed by conducting a job analysis, which includes examining the tasks and sequences of tasks necessary to perform the job.
   a. Recruitment
   b. Job description
   c. Recruitment Process Insourcing
   d. Recruitment advertising

2. _____ refers to a range of skills, tools, and techniques used to manage time when accomplishing specific tasks, projects and goals. This set encompass a wide scope of activities, and these include planning, allocating, setting goals, delegation, analysis of time spent, monitoring, organizing, scheduling, and prioritizing. Initially _____ referred to just business or work activities, but eventually the term broadened to include personal activities also.
   a. Time management
   b. Cash cow
   c. Voice of the customer
   d. Formula for Change

3. _____ generally refers to a list of all planned expenses and revenues. It is a plan for saving and spending. A _____ is an important concept in microeconomics, which uses a _____ line to illustrate the trade-offs between two or more goods.
   a. 28-hour day
   b. 33 Strategies of War
   c. 1990 Clean Air Act
   d. Budget

4. _____ refers to the movement of cash into or out of a business or financial product. It is usually measured during a specified, finite period of time. Measurement of _____ can be used

   - to determine a project's rate of return or value. The time of _____ s into and out of projects are used as inputs in financial models such as internal rate of return, and net present value.
   - to determine problems with a business's liquidity. Being profitable does not necessarily mean being liquid. A company can fail because of a shortage of cash, even while profitable.
   - as an alternate measure of a business's profits when it is believed that accrual accounting concepts do not represent economic realities. For example, a company may be notionally profitable but generating little operational cash (as may be the case for a company that barters its products rather than selling for cash.) In such a case, the company may be deriving additional operating cash by issuing shares evaluating default risk, re-investment requirements, etc.

   _____ is a generic term used differently depending on the context. It may be defined by users for their own purposes.

## Chapter 10. Plans and Planning Techniques: Goals and objectives get you there faster    41

  a. Gross profit margin
  b. Gross profit
  c. Sweat equity
  d. Cash flow


5. _____ is the discipline of planning, organizing and managing resources to bring about the successful completion of specific project goals and objectives. It is often closely related to and sometimes conflated with Program management.

A project is a finite endeavor--having specific start and completion dates--undertaken to meet particular goals and objectives, usually to bring about beneficial change or added value.

  a. Project management
  b. Precedence diagram
  c. Project engineer
  d. Work package


6. _____ are a set of documents that describe an organization's policies for operation and the procedures necessary to fulfill the policies. They are often initiated because of some external requirement, such as environmental compliance or other governmental regulations, such as the American Sarbanes-Oxley Act requiring full openness in accounting practices. The easiest way to start writing _____ is to interview the users of the _____ and create a flow chart or task map or work flow of the process from start to finish.

  a. Customer retention
  b. Horizontal integration
  c. Policies and procedures
  d. Group booking


7. _____ is the process of comparing the cost, cycle time, productivity, or quality of a specific process or method to another that is widely considered to be an industry standard or best practice. Essentially, _____ provides a snapshot of the performance of your business and helps you understand where you are in relation to a particular standard. The result is often a business case for making changes in order to make improvements.

  a. Complementors
  b. Competitive heterogeneity
  c. Cost leadership
  d. Benchmarking


8. _____ is the process of estimation in unknown situations. Prediction is a similar, but more general term. Both can refer to estimation of time series, cross-sectional or longitudinal data.

## Chapter 10. Plans and Planning Techniques: Goals and objectives get you there faster

a. 33 Strategies of War
b. Forecasting
c. 1990 Clean Air Act
d. 28-hour day


9. _____ is a strategic planning method that some organizations use to make flexible long-term plans. It is in large part an adaptation and generalization of classic methods used by military intelligence.

The original method was that a group of analysts would generate simulation games for policy makers. In business applications, the emphasis on gaming the behavior of opponents was reduced (shifting more toward a game against nature). At Royal Dutch/Shell for example, _____ was viewed as changing mindsets about the exogenous part of the world, prior to formulating specific strategies.

a. Scenario planning
b. Time and attendance
c. Labour productivity
d. Retroactive overtime


10. A _____ is the belief that there is a technique, method, process, activity, incentive or reward that is more effective at delivering a particular outcome than any other technique, method, process, etc. The idea is that with proper processes, checks, and testing, a desired outcome can be delivered with fewer problems and unforeseen complications. _____s can also be defined as the most efficient (least amount of effort) and effective (best results) way of accomplishing a task, based on repeatable procedures that have proven themselves over time for large numbers of people.

a. Fix it twice
b. Design management
c. Hierarchical organization
d. Best practice


11. _____ is an urban planning paradigm which emphasizes involving the entire community in the strategic and management processes of urban planning or community-level planning processes, urban or rural. It is often considered as part of community development processes.

In the UN Habitat document Building Bridges Through _____, Fred Fisher, president of the International Development Institute for Organization and Management, identifies Participatory Reflection And Action (PRA) as the leading school of _____.

a. 33 Strategies of War
b. 28-hour day
c. 1990 Clean Air Act
d. Participatory planning

## Chapter 11. Controls and Control Systems: Mat gets measured happens

1. _____ is one of the managerial functions like planning, organizing, staffing and directing. It is an important function because it helps to check the errors and to take the corrective action so that deviation from standards are minimized and stated goals of the organization are achieved in desired manner. According to modern concepts, _____ is a foreseeing action whereas earlier concept of _____ was used only when errors were detected. _____ in management means setting standards, measuring actual performance and taking corrective action.
    a. Control
    b. Schedule of reinforcement
    c. Turnover
    d. Decision tree pruning

2. A _____ is a list of the general tasks and responsibilities of a position. Typically, it also includes to whom the position reports, specifications such as the qualifications needed by the person in the job, salary range for the position, etc. A _____ is usually developed by conducting a job analysis, which includes examining the tasks and sequences of tasks necessary to perform the job.
    a. Recruitment
    b. Recruitment Process Insourcing
    c. Recruitment advertising
    d. Job description

3. 

_____ is a commonly used, yet poorly defined concept in industrial and organizational psychology, the branch of psychology that deals with the workplace. It most commonly refers to whether a person performs their job well. Despite the confusion over how it should be exactly defined, performance is an extremely important criterion that relates to organizational outcomes and success.

   a. 28-hour day
   b. 33 Strategies of War
   c. 1990 Clean Air Act
   d. Job performance

4. _____ is a method by which the job performance of an employee is evaluated _____ is a part of career development.

_____s are regular reviews of employee performance within organizations

Generally, the aims of a _____ are to:

- Give feedback on performance to employees.
- Identify employee training needs.
- Document criteria used to allocate organizational rewards.
- Form a basis for personnel decisions: salary increases, promotions, disciplinary actions, etc.
- Provide the opportunity for organizational diagnosis and development.
- Facilitate communication between employee and administraton
- Validate selection techniques and human resource policies to meet federal Equal Employment Opportunity requirements.

A common approach to assessing performance is to use a numerical or scalar rating system whereby managers are asked to score an individual against a number of objectives/attributes. In some companies, employees receive assessments from their manager, peers, subordinates and customers while also performing a self assessment.

a. Human resource management
b. Personnel management
c. Progressive discipline
d. Performance appraisal


5. _____ describes how content an individual is with his or her job.

The happier people are within their job, the more satisfied they are said to be. _____ is not the same as motivation, although it is clearly linked.

a. Job analysis
b. Goal-setting theory
c. Human relations
d. Job satisfaction


6. _____ describes the situation when output from (or information about the result of) an event or phenomenon in the past will influence the same event/phenomenon in the present or future. When an event is part of a chain of cause-and-effect that forms a circuit or loop, then the event is said to 'feed back' into itself.

## Chapter 11. Controls and Control Systems: Mat gets measured happens

_____ is also a synonym for:

- _____ signal; the information about the initial event that is the basis for subsequent modification of the event.
- _____ loop; the causal path that leads from the initial generation of the _____ signal to the subsequent modification of the event.

_____ is a mechanism, process or signal that is looped back to control a system within itself. Such a loop is called a _____ loop.

a. Positive feedback
b. Feedback loop
c. 1990 Clean Air Act
d. Feedback


7. _____ is a 'policy by which management devotes its time to investigating only those situations in which actual results differ significantly from planned results. The idea is that management should spend its valuable time concentrating on the more important items (such as shaping the company's future strategic course.) Attention is given only to material deviations requiring investigation.'

It is not entirely synonymous with the concept of exception management in that it describes a policy where absolute focus is on exception management, in contrast to moderate application of exception management.

a. Business philosophy
b. C-A-K-E
c. Trustee
d. Management by exception


8. _____ is the process of comparing the cost, cycle time, productivity, or quality of a specific process or method to another that is widely considered to be an industry standard or best practice. Essentially, _____ provides a snapshot of the performance of your business and helps you understand where you are in relation to a particular standard. The result is often a business case for making changes in order to make improvements.

a. Cost leadership
b. Competitive heterogeneity
c. Benchmarking
d. Complementors

## Chapter 11. Controls and Control Systems: Mat gets measured happens

9. _____ is a process of agreeing upon objectives within an organization so that management and employees agree to the objectives and understand what they are in the organization.

The term '_____' was first popularized by Peter Drucker in his 1954 book 'The Practice of Management'.

The essence of _____ is participative goal setting, choosing course of actions and decision making.

a. Job enrichment
b. Business economics
c. Clean sheet review
d. Management by objectives


10. _____ , also referred to simply as a 'public offering' or 'flotation,' is when a company issues common stock or shares to the public for the first time. They are often issued by smaller, younger companies seeking capital to expand, but can also be done by large privately-owned companies looking to become publicly traded.

In an _____ the issuer may obtain the assistance of an underwriting firm, which helps it determine what type of security to issue (common or preferred), best offering price and time to bring it to market.

a. Occupational Safety and Health Administration
b. Initial public offering
c. Outsourcing
d. Unemployment insurance


11. _____ is a system of discipline where the penalties increase upon repeat occurrences.

This term is often used in an employment or human resources context where rather than terminating employees for first or minor infractions, there is a system of escalating responses intended to correct the negative behaviour rather than to punish the employee.

The typical stages of _____ in a workplace are:

1. Counselling or a verbal warning;
2. A written warning;
3. Suspension or demotion; and
4. Termination.

The stage chosen for a particular infraction will depend on a variety of factors that include the severity of the infraction, the previous work history of the employee and how the choice will affect others in the organization.

## Chapter 11. Controls and Control Systems: Mat gets measured happens

   a. Salary
   b. Performance appraisal
   c. Human resource management
   d. Progressive discipline

12. _____ is the level of inventory that minimizes the total inventory holding costs and ordering costs. The framework used to determine this order quantity is also known as Wilson _____ Model. The model was developed by F. W. Harris in 1913.
   a. Effective executive
   b. Event management
   c. Anti-leadership
   d. Economic order quantity

13. _____ is an inventory strategy that strives to improve the return on investment of a business by reducing in-process inventory and its associated carrying costs. To meet _____ objectives, the process relies on signals between different points in the process. This means the process is often driven by a series of signals, or Kanban , which tell production when to make the next part. Kanban are usually 'tickets' but can be simple visual signals, such as the presence or absence of a part on a shelf. Implemented correctly, _____ can dramatically improve a manufacturing organization's return on investment, quality, and efficiency.
   a. 28-hour day
   b. 33 Strategies of War
   c. Just-in-time
   d. 1990 Clean Air Act

14. A _____ is a volunteer group composed of workers (or even students), usually under the leadership of their supervisor (but they can elect a team leader), who are trained to identify, analyse and solve work-related problems and present their solutions to management in order to improve the performance of the organization, and motivate and enrich the work of employees. When matured, true _____s become self-managing, having gained the confidence of management. _____s are an alternative to the dehumanising concept of the Division of Labour, where workers or individuals are treated like robots.
   a. Certified in Production and Inventory Management
   b. Competency-based job descriptions
   c. Connectionist expert systems
   d. Quality circle

## Chapter 11. Controls and Control Systems: Mat gets measured happens

15. A _____ is the system of organizations, people, technology, activities, information and resources involved in moving a product or service from supplier to customer. _____ activities transform natural resources, raw materials and components into a finished product that is delivered to the end customer. In sophisticated _____ systems, used products may re-enter the _____ at any point where residual value is recyclable.

   a. Wholesalers
   b. Supply chain
   c. Packaging
   d. Drop shipping

16. _____ is the management of a network of interconnected businesses involved in the ultimate provision of product and service packages required by end customers (Harland, 1996.) _____ spans all movement and storage of raw materials, work-in-process inventory, and finished goods from point of origin to point of consumption (supply chain.)

   The definition an American professional association put forward is that _____ encompasses the planning and management of all activities involved in sourcing, procurement, conversion, and logistics management activities.

   a. Drop shipping
   b. Freight forwarder
   c. Packaging
   d. Supply chain management

17. _____ is a business management strategy aimed at embedding awareness of quality in all organizational processes. _____ has been widely used in manufacturing, education, hospitals, call centers, government, and service industries, as well as NASA space and science programs.

   As defined by the International Organization for Standardization (ISO):

   '_____ is a management approach for an organization, centered on quality, based on the participation of all its members and aiming at long-term success through customer satisfaction, and benefits to all members of the organization and to society.' ISO 8402:1994

   One major aim is to reduce variation from every process so that greater consistency of effort is obtained. (Royse, D., Thyer, B., Padgett D., ' Logan T., 2006)

   a. Total quality management
   b. 28-hour day
   c. Quality management
   d. 1990 Clean Air Act

18. _____ can be considered to have three main components: quality control, quality assurance and quality improvement. _____ is focused not only on product quality, but also the means to achieve it. _____ therefore uses quality assurance and control of processes as well as products to achieve more consistent quality.

a. 1990 Clean Air Act
b. 28-hour day
c. Total quality management
d. Quality management

## Chapter 12. Strategic Management: Insights and hard work deliver results

1. _____ is, in very basic words, a position a firm occupies against its competitors.

According to Michael Porter, the three methods for creating a sustainable _____ are through:

1. Cost leadership

2. Differentiation

3. Focus (economics)

   a. 1990 Clean Air Act
   b. Theory Z
   c. 28-hour day
   d. Competitive advantage

2. The general definition of an _____ is an evaluation of a person, organization, system, process, project or product. _____s are performed to ascertain the validity and reliability of information; also to provide an assessment of a system's internal control. The goal of an _____ is to express an opinion on the person / organization/system (etc) in question, under evaluation based on work done on a test basis.
   a. A Stake in the Outcome
   b. Audit committee
   c. Internal control
   d. Audit

3. In finance and economics, _____ or divestiture is the reduction of some kind of asset for either financial or ethical objectives or sale of an existing business by a firm. A _____ is the opposite of an investment.
   a. 28-hour day
   b. 33 Strategies of War
   c. 1990 Clean Air Act
   d. Divestment

4. _____ in its literal sense is the process of transformation of local or regional phenomena into global ones. It can be described as a process by which the people of the world are unified into a single society and function together.

This process is a combination of economic, technological, sociocultural and political forces.

a. Histogram
b. Cost Management
c. Collaborative Planning, Forecasting and Replenishment
d. Globalization


5. In law, _____ refers to the process by which a company (or part of a company) is brought to an end, and the assets and property of the company redistributed. _____ can also be referred to as winding-up or dissolution, although dissolution technically refers to the last stage of _____. The process of _____ also arises when customs, an authority or agency in a country responsible for collecting and safeguarding customs duties, determines the final computation or ascertainment of the duties or drawback accruing on an entry.
   a. Liquidation
   b. 1990 Clean Air Act
   c. 33 Strategies of War
   d. 28-hour day


6. _____ is the corporate management term for the act of reorganizing the legal, ownership, operational, or other structures of a company for the purpose of making it more profitable, or better organized for its present needs. Alternate reasons for _____ include a change of ownership or ownership structure, demerger repositioning debt _____ and financial _____.
   a. Net worth
   b. Restructuring
   c. Market value added
   d. Market value


7. In microeconomics and management, the term _____ describes a style of management control. Vertically integrated companies are united through a hierarchy with a common owner. Usually each member of the hierarchy produces a different product or (market-specific) service, and the products combine to satisfy a common need.
   a. Vertical integration
   b. 33 Strategies of War
   c. 1990 Clean Air Act
   d. 28-hour day


8. _____, commonly referred to as 'eBusiness' or 'e-Business', may be defined as the utilization of information and communication technologies (ICT) in support of all the activities of business. Commerce constitutes the exchange of products and services between businesses, groups and individuals and hence can be seen as one of the essential activities of any business. Hence, electronic commerce or eCommerce focuses on the use of ICT to enable the external activities and relationships of the business with individuals, groups and other businesses .

## Chapter 12. Strategic Management: Insights and hard work deliver results 53

   a. AAAI
   b. A Stake in the Outcome
   c. A4e
   d. Electronic business

9. A _____ is a framework for creating economic, social, and/or other forms of value. The term _____ is thus used for a broad range of informal and formal descriptions to represent core aspects of a business, including purpose, offerings, strategies, infrastructure, organizational structures, trading practices, and operational processes and policies.

Conceptualizations of _____s try to formalize informal descriptions into building blocks and their relationships.

   a. Gap analysis
   b. Business model
   c. Business networking
   d. Business model design

10. _____ of the learning curve effect and the closely related experience curve effect express the relationship between equations for experience and efficiency or between efficiency gains and investment in the effort. The experience of 'learning curves' was first observed by the 19th Century German psychologist Hermann Ebbinghaus according to the difficulty of memorizing varying numbers of verbal stimuli, and subsequent learning about the complex processes of learning are discussed in the

.

The rule used for representing the learning curve effect states that the more times a task has been performed, the less time will be required on each subsequent iteration.

   a. Distribution
   b. Point biserial correlation coefficient
   c. Models
   d. Spatial Decision Support Systems

11. _____ is something that a firm can do well and that meets the following three conditions:

Competencies are things that companys execute well across several business units or product sectors.

Firms usually have few competencies, but these are usually less liable to change rapidly.

1. It provides consumer benefits
2. It is not easy for competitors to imitate
3. It can be leveraged widely to many products and markets.

A _____ can take various forms, including technical/subject matter know-how, a reliable process and/or close relationships with customers and suppliers (Mascarenhas et al. 1998.)

   a. NAIRU
   b. Learning-by-doing
   c. Dominant Design
   d. Core competency


12. _____ is a strategic planning method used to evaluate the Strengths, Weaknesses, Opportunities, and Threats involved in a project or in a business venture. It involves specifying the objective of the business venture or project and identifying the internal and external factors that are favorable and unfavorable to achieving that objective. The technique is credited to Albert Humphrey, who led a convention at Stanford University in the 1960s and 1970s using data from Fortune 500 companies.
   a. Corporate image
   b. SWOT analysis
   c. Marketing
   d. Market share


13. In economics, business, retail, and accounting, a _____ is the value of money that has been used up to produce something, and hence is not available for use anymore. In economics, a _____ is an alternative that is given up as a result of a decision. In business, the _____ may be one of acquisition, in which case the amount of money expended to acquire it is counted as _____.
   a. Cost overrun
   b. Cost allocation
   c. Fixed costs
   d. Cost


14. _____ is a concept developed by Michael Porter, used in business strategy. It describes a way to establish the competitive advantage. _____, in basic words, means the lowest cost of operation in the industry.

a. Switching cost
b. Cost leadership
c. Strategic business unit
d. Strategic group


15. _____ has been described as the 'process of social influence in which one person can enlist the aid and support of others in the accomplishment of a common task' . A definition more inclusive of followers comes from Alan Keith of Genentech who said '_____ is ultimately about creating a way for people to contribute to making something extraordinary happen.'

_____ is one of the most salient aspects of the organizational context. However, defining _____ has been challenging.

a. Situational leadership
b. 28-hour day
c. 1990 Clean Air Act
d. Leadership


16. The _____ is a chart that had been created by Bruce Henderson for the Boston Consulting Group in 1970 to help corporations with analyzing their business units or product lines. This helps the company allocate resources and is used as an analytical tool in brand marketing, product management, strategic management, and portfolio analysis. _____

To use the chart, analysts plot a scatter graph to rank the business units (or products) on the basis of their relative market shares and growth rates.

a. Marketing strategy
b. Market segment
c. Marketing plan
d. BCG matrix

## Chapter 13. Organizational Structures: Its all about working together

1. An _____, or organogram(me)) is a diagram that shows the structure of an organization and the relationships and relative ranks of its parts and positions/jobs. The term is also used for similar diagrams, for example ones showing the different elements of a field of knowledge or a group of languages. The French Encyclopédie had one of the first _____s of knowledge in general.
    a. A4e
    b. AAAI
    c. A Stake in the Outcome
    d. Organizational chart

2. A _____ is a list of the general tasks and responsibilities of a position. Typically, it also includes to whom the position reports, specifications such as the qualifications needed by the person in the job, salary range for the position, etc. A _____ is usually developed by conducting a job analysis, which includes examining the tasks and sequences of tasks necessary to perform the job.
    a. Recruitment Process Insourcing
    b. Job description
    c. Recruitment
    d. Recruitment advertising

3. The _____ is the interlocking social structure that governs how people work together in practice. It is the aggregate of behaviors, interactions, norms, personal and professional connections through which work gets done and relationships are built among people who share a common organizational affiliation or cluster of affiliations. It consists of a dynamic set of personal relationships, social networks, communities of common interest, and emotional sources of motivation. The _____ evolves organically and spontaneously in response to changes in the work environment, the flux of people through its porous boundaries, and the complex social dynamics of its members.
    a. Organizational effectiveness
    b. Union shop
    c. Open shop
    d. Informal Organization

4. _____ refers to the process of grouping activities into departments.

Division of labour creates specialists who need coordination. This coordination is facilitated by grouping specialists together in departments.

    a. Departmentalization
    b. Division of labour
    c. Maximum wage
    d. Decent work

## Chapter 13. Organizational Structures: Its all about working together

5. _____ is a type of organizational management in which people with similar skills are pooled for work assignments. For example, all engineers may be in one engineering department and report to an engineering manager, but these same engineers may be assigned to different projects and report to a project manager while working on that project. Therefore, each engineer may have to work under several managers to get their job done.

   a. Span of control
   b. Management development
   c. Central Administration
   d. Matrix management

6. A _____ is a group of employees from various functional areas of the organization - research, engineering, marketing, finance. human resources, and operations, for example - who are all focused on a specific objective and are responsible to work as a team to improve coordination and innovation across divisions and resolve mutual problems.

   a. Sociotechnical systems
   b. Goal-setting theory
   c. Graduate recruitment
   d. Cross-functional team

7. _____ is subcontracting a process, such as product design or manufacturing, to a third-party company. The decision to outsource is often made in the interest of lowering cost or making better use of time and energy costs, redirecting or conserving energy directed at the competencies of a particular business, or to make more efficient use of land, labor, capital, (information) technology and resources. _____ became part of the business lexicon during the 1980s.

   a. Unemployment insurance
   b. Operant conditioning
   c. Outsourcing
   d. Opinion leadership

8. A _____ is a formal relationship between two or more parties to pursue a set of agreed upon goals or to meet a critical business need while remaining independent organizations.

   Partners may provide the _____ with resources such as products, distribution channels, manufacturing capability, project funding, capital equipment, knowledge, expertise, or intellectual property. The alliance is a cooperation or collaboration which aims for a synergy where each partner hopes that the benefits from the alliance will be greater than those from individual efforts.

   a. Strategic alliance
   b. Process automation
   c. Golden parachute
   d. Farmshoring

## Chapter 14. Organizational Design and Culture: Adaptability and values set the tone

1. _____ is the process by which the activities of an organisation, particularly those regarding decision-making, become concentrated within a particular location and/or group.
    a. Corner office
    b. Chief operating officer
    c. Product innovation
    d. Centralization

2. _____ is the process of dispersing decision-making governance closer to the people or citizen. It includes the dispersal of administration or governance in sectors or areas like engineering, management science, political science, political economy, sociology and economics. _____ is also possible in the dispersal of population and employment.
    a. Formula for Change
    b. Decentralization
    c. Frenemy
    d. Business plan

3. _____ is a term originating in military organization theory, but now used more commonly in business management, particularly human resource management. _____ refers to the number of subordinates a supervisor has.

In the hierarchical business organization of the past it was not uncommon to see average spans of 1 to 10 or even less. That is, one manager supervised ten employees on average.

    a. CIFMS
    b. Senior management
    c. Span of control
    d. Mentoring

4. _____ is one of the managerial functions like planning, organizing, staffing and directing. It is an important function because it helps to check the errors and to take the corrective action so that deviation from standards are minimized and stated goals of the organization are achieved in desired manner. According to modern concepts, _____ is a foreseeing action whereas earlier concept of _____ was used only when errors were detected. _____ in management means setting standards, measuring actual performance and taking corrective action.
    a. Control
    b. Turnover
    c. Schedule of reinforcement
    d. Decision tree pruning

5. _____ refers to increasing the spiritual, political, social or economic strength of individuals and communities. It often involves the empowered developing confidence in their own capacities.

## Chapter 14. Organizational Design and Culture: Adaptability and values set the tone

The term Human _____ covers a vast landscape of meanings, interpretations, definitions and disciplines ranging from psychology and philosophy to the highly commercialized Self-Help industry and Motivational sciences.

a. A4e
b. AAAI
c. A Stake in the Outcome
d. Empowerment

6. In management science, operations research and organizational development (OD), human organizations are viewed as systems (conceptual systems) of interacting components such as _____ or system aggregates, which are carriers of numerous complex processes and organizational structures. Organizational development theorist Peter Senge developed the notion of organizations as systems in his book The Fifth Discipline.

Systems thinking is a style of thinking/reasoning and problem solving.

a. Subsystems
b. Systems thinking
c. 28-hour day
d. 1990 Clean Air Act

7. _____ is an idea in the field of Organizational studies and management which describes the psychology, attitudes, experiences, beliefs and Values (personal and cultural values) of an organization. It has been defined as 'the specific collection of values and norms that are shared by people and groups in an organization and that control the way they interact with each other and with stakeholders outside the organization.'

This definition continues to explain organizational values also known as 'beliefs and ideas about what kinds of goals members of an organization should pursue and ideas about the appropriate kinds or standards of behavior organizational members should use to achieve these goals. From organizational values develop organizational norms, guidelines or expectations that prescribe appropriate kinds of behavior by employees in particular situations and control the behavior of organizational members towards one another.'

_____ is not the same as corporate culture.

a. Organizational development
b. Organizational effectiveness
c. Union shop
d. Organizational culture

## Chapter 15. Human Resource Management: Nuturing turns potential into performance

1. The terms _____ and positive action refer to policies that take race, ethnicity, or gender into consideration in an attempt to promote equal opportunity. The focus of such policies ranges from employment and education to public contracting and health programs. The impetus towards _____ is twofold: to maximize diversity in all levels of society, along with its presumed benefits, and to redress perceived disadvantages due to overt, institutional, or involuntary discrimination.

   a. Affiliation
   b. Abraham Harold Maslow
   c. Adam Smith
   d. Affirmative action

2. The _____ was a landmark piece of legislation in the United States that outlawed racial segregation in schools, public places, and employment.
   a. Civil Rights Act of 1964
   b. Financial Security Law of France
   c. Negligence in employment
   d. Design patent

3. _____ is a contract between two parties, one being the employer and the other being the employee. An employee may be defined as: 'A person in the service of another under any contract of hire, express or implied, oral or written, where the employer has the power or right to control and direct the employee in the material details of how the work is to be performed.' Black's Law Dictionary page 471 (5th ed. 1979.)
   a. Employment counsellor
   b. Employment rate
   c. Exit interview
   d. Employment

4. The term _____ was created by President Lyndon B. Johnson when he signed Executive Order 11246 on September 24, 1965, created to prohibit federal contractors from discriminating against employees on the basis of race, sex, creed, religion, color, or national origin. In more recent times, most employers have also added sexual orientation to the list of non-discrimination.

The Executive Order also required contractors to implement affirmative action plans to increase the participation of minorities and women in the workplace.

*Chapter 15. Human Resource Management: Nuturing turns potential into performance*   61

   a. A4e
   b. A Stake in the Outcome
   c. AAAI
   d. Equal Employment Opportunity


5. _____ is the strategic and coherent approach to the management of an organisation's most valued assets - the people working there who individually and collectively contribute to the achievement of the objectives of the business. The terms '_____' and 'human resources' (HR) have largely replaced the term 'personnel management' as a description of the processes involved in managing people in organizations. In simple sense, _____ means employing people, developing their resources, utilizing, maintaining and compensating their services in tune with the job and organizational requirement.
   a. Job knowledge
   b. Revolving door syndrome
   c. Progressive discipline
   d. Human resource management


6. The _____ of 1967, Pub. L. No. 90-202, 81 Stat. 602 (Dec. 15, 1967), codified as Chapter 14 of Title 29 of the United States Code, 29 U.S.C. § 621 through 29 U.S.C. § 634 (ADEA), prohibits employment discrimination against persons 40 years of age or older in the United States ). The law also sets standards for pensions and benefits provided by employers and requires that information about the needs of older workers be provided to the general public.
   a. Undue hardship
   b. Extra time
   c. Unemployment and Farm Relief Act
   d. Age Discrimination in Employment Act


7. The _____ of 1990 (ADA) is the short title of United States (Pub.L. 101-336, 104 Stat. 327, enacted July 26, 1990), codified at 42 U.S.C. § 12101 et seq. It was signed into law on July 26, 1990, by President George H. W. Bush, and later amended with changes effective January 1, 2009. The ADA is a wide-ranging civil rights law that prohibits, under certain circumstances, discrimination based on disability. It affords similar protections against discrimination to Americans with disabilities as the Civil Rights Act of 1964,
   a. Equal Pay Act of 1963
   b. Employment discrimination
   c. Australian labour law
   d. Americans with Disabilities Act


8. In employment law, a (BFOQ) (US) or bona fide occupational requirement (BFOR) (Canada) is a quality or an attribute that employers are allowed to consider when making decisions on the hiring and retention of employees - qualities that, when considered, in other contexts would be considered discriminatory and thus violating civil rights employment law.

In employment discrimination law in the United States, United States Code Title 29, Chapter 14 (age discrimination in employment), section 623 (prohibition of age discrimination) establishes that 'It shall not be unlawful for an employer, employment agency, or labor organization (1) to take any action otherwise prohibited under subsections (a), (b), (c), or (e) of this section where age is a _____ reasonably necessary to the normal operation of the particular business, or where the differentiation is based on reasonable factors other than age, or where such practices involve an employee in a workplace in a foreign country, and compliance with such subsections would cause such employer, or a corporation controlled by such employer, to violate the laws of the country in which such workplace is located.'

One example of _____s are mandatory retirement ages for bus drivers and airline pilots, for safety reasons. Further, in advertising, a manufacturer of men's clothing may lawfully advertise for male models.

a. Corporate governance
b. Bona fide occupational qualification
c. MacPherson v. Buick Motor Co.
d. Sick leave

9. The _____ is a United States statute that was passed in response to a series of United States Supreme Court decisions which limited the rights of employees who had sued their employers for discrimination. The Act represented the first effort since the passage of the Civil Rights Act of 1964 to modify some of the basic procedural and substantive rights provided by federal law in employment discrimination cases. It provided for the right to trial by jury on discrimination claims and introduced the possibility of emotional distress damages, while limiting the amount that a jury could award

The 1991 Act combined elements from two different civil rights acts of the past: the Civil Rights Act of 1866, better known by the number assigned to it in the codification of federal laws as 'Section 1981', and the employment-related provisions of the Civil Rights Act of 1964, generally referred to as 'Title VII', its location within the Act.

a. Negligence in employment
b. Resource Conservation and Recovery Act
c. Covenant
d. Civil Rights Act of 1991

10. The _____ 1970 is an Act of the United Kingdom Parliament which prohibits any less favourable treatment between men and women in terms of pay and conditions of employment. It came into force on 29 December 1975. The term pay is interpreted in a broad sense to include, on top of wages, things like holidays, pension rights, company perks and some kinds of bonuses.

a. Australian labour law
b. Oncale v. Sundowner Offshore Services
c. Architectural Barriers Act of 1968
d. Equal Pay Act


11. The _____ is a United States labor law allowing an employee to take unpaid leave due to a serious health condition that makes the employee unable to perform his job or to care for a sick family member or to care for a new son or daughter (including by birth, adoption or foster care.) The bill was among the first signed into law by President Bill Clinton in his first term.
   a. Sarbanes-Oxley Act of 2002
   b. Harvester Judgment
   c. Contributory negligence
   d. Family and Medical Leave Act of 1993


12. _____ occurs when expectant women are fired, not hired, or otherwise discriminated against due to their pregnancy or intention to become pregnant. Common forms of _____ include not being hired due to visible pregnancy or likelihood of becoming pregnant, being fired after informing an employer of one's pregnancy, being fired after maternity leave, and receiving a pay dock due to pregnancy. In the United States, since 1978, employers are legally bound to provide what insurance, leave pay, and additional support that would be bestowed upon any employee with medical leave or disability.
   a. 28-hour day
   b. 33 Strategies of War
   c. 1990 Clean Air Act
   d. Pregnancy Discrimination


13. _____ is, in its simplest form, the practice of favoring members of a historically disadvantaged group at the expense of members of a historically advantaged group.

In the United States, the terms '_____' and 'reverse racism' have been used in past discussions of racial quotas or gender quotas for collegiate admission to government-run educational institutions. Such policies were held to be unconstitutional in the United States, while non-quota race preferences are legal.

   a. Sexism,
   b. 1990 Clean Air Act
   c. Separate but equal
   d. Reverse discrimination

## Chapter 15. Human Resource Management: Nuturing turns potential into performance

14. An _____ is a natural person, business, or corporation which provides goods or services to another entity under terms specified in a contract or within a verbal agreement. Unlike an employee, an _____ does not work regularly for an employer but works as and when required, during which time she or he may be subject to the Law of Agency. _____s are usually paid on a freelance basis.
   a. Equal Pay Act of 1963
   b. Independent contractor
   c. Employment protection legislation
   d. Occupational Safety and Health Act

15. _____ is the body of laws, administrative rulings, and precedents which address the legal rights of, and restrictions on, working people and their organizations. As such, it mediates many aspects of the relationship between trade unions, employers and employees. In Canada, employment laws related to unionized workplaces are differentiated from those relating to particular individuals.
   a. Four-day week
   b. Trade union
   c. Labor law
   d. Shift work

16. A _____ or labor union is an organization of workers who have banded together to achieve common goals in key areas and working conditions. The _____, through its leadership, bargains with the employer on behalf of union members (rank and file members) and negotiates labor contracts (Collective bargaining) with employers. This may include the negotiation of wages, work rules, complaint procedures, rules governing hiring, firing and promotion of workers, benefits, workplace safety and policies.
   a. Labour law
   b. Company union
   c. Trade union
   d. Working time

17. A _____ is an employee whose status is somewhere between a temporary employee and a permanent employee. The word is a portmanteau of the words permanent and temporary. It is sort of a tongue-in-cheek textual contrivance poking fun at the dynamics of the New Economy with its characteristic job insecurity and lack of benefits for a considerable portion of the workforce.
   a. Permatemp
   b. Work experience
   c. Job fraud
   d. Career Pathways

## Chapter 15. Human Resource Management: Nuturing turns potential into performance    65

18. Employees typically must relinquish some of their _____, but how much they must do so can be a contentious issue. Employers might choose to monitor employees activities using surveillance cameras, or may wish to record employees activities while using company owned computers or telephones.

The EU Directive 95/46/EC on the protection of individuals with regard to the processing of personal data and on the free movement of such data limits and regulates the collection of personal information on individuals, including workers.

a. Complement
b. Privacy while at the workplace
c. Job security through obscurity
d. Procter ' Gamble


19. In organized labor, _____ is the method whereby workers organize together (usually in unions) to meet, converse, and negotiate upon the work conditions with their employers normally resulting in a written contract setting forth the wages, hours, and other conditions to be observed for a stipulated period.It is the practice in which union and company representatives meet to negotiate a new labor contract. In various national labor and employment law contexts, the term _____ takes on a more specific legal meaning. In a broad sense, however, it is the coming together of workers to negotiate their employment.

a. Labour law
b. Collective bargaining
c. Paid time off
d. Labor rights


20. _____ is an increasingly broadening term with which an organization, or other human system describes the combination of traditionally administrative personnel functions with acquisition and application of skills, knowledge and experience, Employee Relations and resource planning at various levels. The field draws upon concepts developed in Industrial/Organizational Psychology and System Theory. _____ has at least two related interpretations depending on context. The original usage derives from political economy and economics, where it was traditionally called labor, one of four factors of production although this perspective is changing as a function of new and ongoing research into more strategic approaches at national levels. This first usage is used more in terms of '_____ development', and can go beyond just organizations to the level of nations . The more traditional usage within corporations and businesses refers to the individuals within a firm or agency, and to the portion of the organization that deals with hiring, firing, training, and other personnel issues, typically referred to as `_____ management'.

a. Progressive discipline
b. Human resources
c. Human resource management
d. Bradford Factor

## Chapter 15. Human Resource Management: Nuturing turns potential into performance

21. _____ refers to the process of screening, and selecting qualified people for a job at an organization or firm mid- and large-size organizations and companies often retain professional recruiters or outsource some of the process to _____ agencies. External _____ is the process of attracting and selecting employees from outside the organization.

The _____ industry has four main types of agencies: employment agencies, _____ websites and job search engines, 'headhunters' for executive and professional _____, and in-house _____.

   a. Recruitment
   b. Referral recruitment
   c. Labour hire
   d. Recruitment Process Outsourcing


22. _____ is a form of corporate self-regulation integrated into a business model. Ideally, _____ policy would function as a built-in, self-regulating mechanism whereby business would monitor and ensure their adherence to law, ethical standards, and international norms. Business would embrace responsibility for the impact of their activities on the environment, consumers, employees, communities, stakeholders and all other members of the public sphere.

   a. 33 Strategies of War
   b. 1990 Clean Air Act
   c. 28-hour day
   d. Corporate social responsibility


23. The term _____ in logic applies to arguments or statements.

An argument is valid if and only if the truth of its premises entails the truth of its conclusion, it would be self-contradictory to affirm the premises and deny the conclusion. The corresponding conditional of a valid argument is a logical truth and the negation of its corresponding conditional is a contradiction.

   a. Validity
   b. Fuzzy logic
   c. 1990 Clean Air Act
   d. Simplification


24. A _____ is a process in which a potential employee is evaluated by an employer for prospective employment in their company, organization and was established in the late 16th century.

A _____ typically precedes the hiring decision, and is used to evaluate the candidate. The interview is usually preceded by the evaluation of submitted résumés from interested candidates, then selecting a small number of candidates for interviews.

## Chapter 15. Human Resource Management: Nuturing turns potential into performance

a. Split shift
b. Job interview
c. Supported employment
d. Payrolling

25. There are two types of _____ relationships: formal and informal. Informal relationships develop on their own between partners. Formal _____, on the other hand, refers to assigned relationships, often associated with organizational _____ programs designed to promote employee development or to assist at-risk children and youth.
a. Fix it twice
b. Human resource management system
c. Real Property Administrator
d. Mentoring

26. _____ is a method by which the job performance of an employee is evaluated _____ is a part of career development.

_____s are regular reviews of employee performance within organizations

Generally, the aims of a _____ are to:

- Give feedback on performance to employees.
- Identify employee training needs.
- Document criteria used to allocate organizational rewards.
- Form a basis for personnel decisions: salary increases, promotions, disciplinary actions, etc.
- Provide the opportunity for organizational diagnosis and development.
- Facilitate communication between employee and administraton
- Validate selection techniques and human resource policies to meet federal Equal Employment Opportunity requirements.

A common approach to assessing performance is to use a numerical or scalar rating system whereby managers are asked to score an individual against a number of objectives/attributes. In some companies, employees receive assessments from their manager, peers, subordinates and customers while also performing a self assessment.

a. Human resource management
b. Personnel management
c. Progressive discipline
d. Performance appraisal

## Chapter 15. Human Resource Management: Nuturing turns potential into performance

27. _____ describes the situation when output from (or information about the result of) an event or phenomenon in the past will influence the same event/phenomenon in the present or future. When an event is part of a chain of cause-and-effect that forms a circuit or loop, then the event is said to 'feed back' into itself.

_____ is also a synonym for:

- _____ signal; the information about the initial event that is the basis for subsequent modification of the event.
- _____ loop; the causal path that leads from the initial generation of the _____ signal to the subsequent modification of the event.

_____ is a mechanism, process or signal that is looped back to control a system within itself. Such a loop is called a _____ loop.

a. Positive feedback
b. 1990 Clean Air Act
c. Feedback loop
d. Feedback

28. A _____ is a set of categories designed to elicit information about a quantitative or a qualitative attribute. In the social sciences, common examples are the Likert scale and 1-10 _____s in which a person selects the number which is considered to reflect the perceived quality of a product.

A _____ is an instrument that requires the rater to assign the rated object that have numerals assigned to them.

a. Thurstone scale
b. Rating scale
c. Spearman-Brown prediction formula
d. Polytomous Rasch model

29. _____ is a term defined by the Oxford English Dictionary as an individual's 'course or progress through life '. It is usually considered to pertain to remunerative work (and sometimes also formal education.)

The etymology of the term is somewhat ironic in that it comes from the Latin word carrera, which means race .

## Chapter 15. Human Resource Management: Nuturing turns potential into performance 69

a. Nursing shortage
b. Spatial mismatch
c. Career planning
d. Career


30. In organizational development (or OD), the study of _____ looks at:

    - how individuals manage their careers within and between organizations
    - and how organizations structure the career progress of their members, it can also be tied into succession planning within some organizations.

In personal development, _____ is:

    - '... the total constellation of psychological, sociological, educational, physical, economic, and chance factors that combine to influence the nature and significance of work in the total lifespan of any given individual.'

    - '... the lifelong psychological and behavioral processes as well as contextual influences shaping one's career over the life span. As such, _____ involves the person's creation of a career pattern, decision-making style, integration of life roles, values expression, and life-role self concepts.'

Figures in _____

    - Jeff A. Brown
    - Jesse B. Davis
    - Caela Farren
    - John L. Holland
    - Kris Magnusson
    - Frank Parsons
    - Vance Peavy
    - Edgar Schein
    - Rino Schreuder
    - Mark L. Savickas
    - Donald Super


a. Business process reengineering
b. Sole proprietorship
c. Career development
d. Horizontal integration

31. _____ is a subset of career management. _____ applies the concepts of Strategic planning and Marketing to taking charge of one's professional future.
   a. TDY
   b. Forced retention
   c. Military recruitment
   d. Career planning

## Chapter 16. Leadership: A leader lives in each of us

1. _____ has been described as the 'process of social influence in which one person can enlist the aid and support of others in the accomplishment of a common task'. A definition more inclusive of followers comes from Alan Keith of Genentech who said '_____ is ultimately about creating a way for people to contribute to making something extraordinary happen.'

   _____ is one of the most salient aspects of the organizational context. However, defining _____ has been challenging.

   a. 28-hour day
   b. 1990 Clean Air Act
   c. Situational leadership
   d. Leadership


2. A _____ is a list of the general tasks and responsibilities of a position. Typically, it also includes to whom the position reports, specifications such as the qualifications needed by the person in the job, salary range for the position, etc. A _____ is usually developed by conducting a job analysis, which includes examining the tasks and sequences of tasks necessary to perform the job.
   a. Recruitment
   b. Job description
   c. Recruitment advertising
   d. Recruitment Process Insourcing


3. The _____ is a leadership theory in the field of organizational studies developed by Robert House in 1971 and revised in 1996. The theory that a leader's behavior is contingent to the satisfaction, motivation and performance of subordinates. The revised version also argues that the leader engage in behaviors that complement subordinate's abilities and compensate for deficiencies.
   a. Corporate Culture
   b. Sociotechnical systems
   c. Human relations
   d. Path-goal theory


4. _____ is individual power based on a high level of identification with, admiration of, or respect for the powerholder.

   Nationalism, Patriotism, Celebrities and well-respected people are examples of _____ in effect.

   _____ is one of the Five Bases of Social Power, as defined by Bertram Raven and his colleagues[1] in 1959.

a. 33 Strategies of War
b. 1990 Clean Air Act
c. Referent power
d. 28-hour day

5. _____ is a term used to describe a policy of allowing events to take their own course. The term is a French phrase literally meaning 'let do'. It is a doctrine that states that government generally should not intervene in the marketplace.
   a. Libertarian
   b. Freedom of contract
   c. Laissez-faire
   d. Deep ecology

6. _____ is a term used to classify a group leadership theories that inquire the interactions between leaders and followers. A transactional leader focuses more on a series of 'transactions'. This person is interested in looking out for oneself, having exchange benefits with their subordinates and clarify a sense of duty with rewards and punishments to reach goals.
   a. 28-hour day
   b. 1990 Clean Air Act
   c. 33 Strategies of War
   d. Transactional leadership

7. _____ is a leadership style that defines as leadership that creates voluble and positive change in the followers. A transformational leader focuses on 'transforming' others to help each other, to look out for each other, be encouraging, harmonious, and look out for the organization as a whole. In this leadership, the leader enhances the motivation, moral and performance of his follower group.
   a. Polynomial conjoint measurement
   b. Strong-Campbell Interest Inventory
   c. SESAMO
   d. Transformational leadership

8. _____ , often measured as an _____ Quotient (EQ), is a term that describes the ability, capacity, skill or (in the case of the trait _____ model) a self-perceived ability, to identify, assess, and manage the emotions of one's self, of others, and of groups. Different models have been proposed for the definition of _____ and disagreement exists as to how the term should be used. Despite these disagreements, which are often highly technical, the ability _____ and trait _____ models (but not the mixed models) are enjoying considerable support in the literature and have successful applications in many different domains.

a. AAAI
b. A4e
c. Emotional intelligence
d. A Stake in the Outcome



9. _____ refers to increasing the spiritual, political, social or economic strength of individuals and communities. It often involves the empowered developing confidence in their own capacities.

The term Human _____ covers a vast landscape of meanings, interpretations, definitions and disciplines ranging from psychology and philosophy to the highly commercialized Self-Help industry and Motivational sciences.

a. A Stake in the Outcome
b. Empowerment
c. AAAI
d. A4e


10. _____ is an approach to leadership development, coined and defined by Robert Greenleaf and advanced by several authors such as Stephen Covey, Peter Block, Peter Senge, Max DePree, Margaret Wheatley, Ken Blanchard, and others. Servant-leadership emphasizes the leader's role as steward of the resources (human, financial and otherwise) provided by the organization. It encourages leaders to serve others while staying focused on achieving results in line with the organization's values and integrity.

a. Abraham Harold Maslow
b. Adam Smith
c. Servant leadership
d. Affiliation

## Chapter 17. Communication: Listening can be the key to understanding

1. _____ is a form of social influence. It is the process of guiding people and oneself toward the adoption of an idea, attitude, or action by rational and symbolic (though not always logical) means. It is strategy of problem-solving relying on 'appeals' rather than coercion.

   a. Self-enhancement
   b. Personal space
   c. Social loafing
   d. Persuasion

2. _____ describes the situation when output from (or information about the result of) an event or phenomenon in the past will influence the same event/phenomenon in the present or future. When an event is part of a chain of cause-and-effect that forms a circuit or loop, then the event is said to 'feed back' into itself.

   _____ is also a synonym for:

   - _____ signal; the information about the initial event that is the basis for subsequent modification of the event.
   - _____ loop; the causal path that leads from the initial generation of the _____ signal to the subsequent modification of the event.

   _____ is a mechanism, process or signal that is looped back to control a system within itself. Such a loop is called a _____ loop.

   a. Feedback
   b. 1990 Clean Air Act
   c. Feedback loop
   d. Positive feedback

3. The term _____ was introduced by anthropologist Edward T. Hall in 1966 to describe set measurable distances between people as they interact. The effects of _____, according to Hall, can be summarized by the following loose rule:

   According to Jonathon Tabor distance-spacing theories based on the early animal-like human of German zoologist Heini Hediger, as found in his 1955 book Studies of the Behavior of Captive Animals in Zoos and Circuses. Hediger, in animals, had distinguished between flight distance , critical distance (attack boundary), personal distance (distance separating members of non-contact species, as a pair of swans), and social distance (intraspecies communication distance.)

   a. 28-hour day
   b. 33 Strategies of War
   c. 1990 Clean Air Act
   d. Proxemics

## Chapter 18. Individual Behavior: There`s beauty in individual differences

1. The trait of _____ is a central dimension of human personality. Extraverts (also spelled extroverts) tend to be gregarious, assertive, and interested in seeking out excitement. Introverts, in contrast, tend to be more reserved, less outgoing, and less sociable.
   a. Extraversion-introversion
   b. AAAI
   c. A Stake in the Outcome
   d. A4e

2. _____ is a term in psychology which refers to a person's belief about what causes the good or bad results in his or her life, either in general or in a specific area such as health or academics. Understanding of the concept was developed by Julian B. Rotter in 1954, and has since become an important aspect of personality studies.

   _____ refers to the extent to which individuals believe that they can control events that affect them.

   a. Social loafing
   b. Machiavellianism
   c. Self-enhancement
   d. Locus of control

3. _____ is one of the managerial functions like planning, organizing, staffing and directing. It is an important function because it helps to check the errors and to take the corrective action so that deviation from standards are minimized and stated goals of the organization are achieved in desired manner. According to modern concepts, _____ is a foreseeing action whereas earlier concept of _____ was used only when errors were detected. _____ in management means setting standards, measuring actual performance and taking corrective action.
   a. Schedule of reinforcement
   b. Turnover
   c. Decision tree pruning
   d. Control

4. _____ , often measured as an _____ Quotient (EQ), is a term that describes the ability, capacity, skill or (in the case of the trait _____ model) a self-perceived ability, to identify, assess, and manage the emotions of one's self, of others, and of groups. Different models have been proposed for the definition of _____ and disagreement exists as to how the term should be used. Despite these disagreements, which are often highly technical, the ability _____ and trait _____ models (but not the mixed models) are enjoying considerable support in the literature and have successful applications in many different domains.
   a. Emotional intelligence
   b. A4e
   c. AAAI
   d. A Stake in the Outcome

## Chapter 18. Individual Behavior: There`s beauty in individual differences

5. _____ is, according to the OED, 'the employment of cunning and duplicity in statecraft or in general conduct', deriving from the Italian Renaissance diplomat and writer Niccolò Machiavelli, who wrote Il Principe and other works. Machiavellian and variants became very popular in the late 16th century in English, though '_____' itself is first cited by the OED from 1626. The word has a similar use in modern psychology.

   a. Machiavellianism
   b. Self-enhancement
   c. Personal space
   d. Persuasion

6. The _____ is a personality type theory that describes a pattern of behaviors that were once considered to be a risk factor for coronary heart disease. Since its inception in the 1950s, the theory has been widely popularized and also widely criticised for its scientific shortcomings.

   Type A individuals can be described as impatient, excessively time-conscious, insecure about their status, highly competitive, over-ambitious, business-like, hostile, aggressive, incapable of relaxation in taking the smallest issues too seriously; and are somewhat disliked for the way that they're always rushing and demanding other people to serve to their standards of satisfaction.

   a. 1990 Clean Air Act
   b. Type A and Type B personality theory
   c. 33 Strategies of War
   d. 28-hour day

7. The _____ refers to a cognitive bias whereby the perception of a particular trait is influenced by the perception of the former traits in a sequence of interpretations.

   Edward L. Thorndike was the first to support the _____ with empirical research. In a psychology study published in 1920, Thorndike asked commanding officers to rate their soldiers; Thorndike found high cross-correlation between all positive and all negative traits.

   a. Halo effect
   b. Distinction bias
   c. Sunk costs
   d. Cognitive biases

## Chapter 18. Individual Behavior: There's beauty in individual differences

8. In attribution theory, the _____ is a theory describing cognitive tendency to predominantly over-value dispositional explanations for the observed behaviors of others, thus under-valuing or acknowledging the potentiality of situational attributions or situational explanations for the behavioral motives of others. In other words, people predominantly presume that the actions of others are indicative of the 'kind' of person they are, rather than the kind of situations that compels their behavior. However, the over attribution effect generally does not account for our own ability to self-justify our behaviors; we tend to prefer interpreting our own actions in terms of the situational variables accessible to our awareness.
   a. Pygmalion effect
   b. Fundamental attribution error
   c. Halo effect
   d. Confirmation bias

9. In sociology and social psychology, _____ is the process through which people try to control the impressions other people form of them. It is a goal-directed conscious or unconscious attempt to influence the perceptions of other people about a person, object or event by regulating and controlling information in social interaction. It is usually used synonymously with self-presentation, if a person tries to influence the perception of their image.
   a. A4e
   b. Impression management
   c. A Stake in the Outcome
   d. AAAI

10. A _____ occurs when people attribute their successes to internal or personal factors but attribute their failures to situational factors beyond their control. The _____ can be seen in the common human tendency to take credit for success but to deny responsibility for failure. It may also manifest itself as a tendency for people to evaluate ambiguous information in a way that is beneficial to their interests.
    a. Fundamental attribution error
    b. Self-serving bias
    c. Halo effect
    d. Pygmalion effect

11. _____ is an uncomfortable feeling caused by holding two contradictory ideas simultaneously. The 'ideas' or 'cognitions' in question may include attitudes and beliefs, and also the awareness of one's behavior. The theory of _____ proposes that people have a motivational drive to reduce dissonance by changing their attitudes, beliefs, and behaviors, or by justifying or rationalizing their attitudes, beliefs, and behaviors.
    a. Cognitive dissonance
    b. Quantitative psychology
    c. Trait theory
    d. Cognitive bias

## Chapter 18. Individual Behavior: There's beauty in individual differences

12. _____ describes how content an individual is with his or her job.

The happier people are within their job, the more satisfied they are said to be. _____ is not the same as motivation, although it is clearly linked.

a. Human relations
b. Job satisfaction
c. Job analysis
d. Goal-setting theory

13.

_____ is a commonly used, yet poorly defined concept in industrial and organizational psychology, the branch of psychology that deals with the workplace. It most commonly refers to whether a person performs their job well. Despite the confusion over how it should be exactly defined, performance is an extremely important criterion that relates to organizational outcomes and success.

a. 28-hour day
b. 1990 Clean Air Act
c. 33 Strategies of War
d. Job performance

14. _____ is a method by which the job performance of an employee is evaluated _____ is a part of career development.

_____s are regular reviews of employee performance within organizations

Generally, the aims of a _____ are to:

- Give feedback on performance to employees.
- Identify employee training needs.
- Document criteria used to allocate organizational rewards.
- Form a basis for personnel decisions: salary increases, promotions, disciplinary actions, etc.
- Provide the opportunity for organizational diagnosis and development.
- Facilitate communication between employee and administraton
- Validate selection techniques and human resource policies to meet federal Equal Employment Opportunity requirements.

A common approach to assessing performance is to use a numerical or scalar rating system whereby managers are asked to score an individual against a number of objectives/attributes. In some companies, employees receive assessments from their manager, peers, subordinates and customers while also performing a self assessment.

a. Personnel management
b. Human resource management
c. Performance appraisal
d. Progressive discipline

# Chapter 19. Motivation: Treat others as you would like to be treated

1. Clayton Paul Alderfer is an American psychologist who further expanded Maslow's hierarchy of needs by categorizing the hierarchy into his _____ Alderfer categorized the lower order needs (Physiological and Safety) into the Existence category. He fit Maslow's interpersonal love and esteem needs into the relatedness category. The growth category contained the Self Actualization and self esteem needs.

   Alderfer also proposed a regression theory to go along with the _____. He said that when needs in a higher category are not met then individuals redouble the efforts invested in a lower category need.

   a. ERG theory
   b. Alvin Neill Jackson
   c. Adam Smith
   d. Abraham Harold Maslow

2. _____ is a term that has been used in various psychology theories, often in slightly different ways (e.g., Goldstein, Maslow, Rogers.) The term was originally introduced by the organismic theorist Kurt Goldstein for the motive to realise all of one's potentialities. In his view, it is the master motive--indeed, the only real motive a person has, all others being merely manifestations of it.
   a. 1990 Clean Air Act
   b. 28-hour day
   c. Self-actualization
   d. 33 Strategies of War

3. _____ are job factors that can cause dissatisfaction if missing but do not necessarily motivate employees if increased.

   _____ have mostly to do with the job environment. These factors are important or notable only when they are lacking.

   a. Split shift
   b. Work system
   c. Work-at-home scheme
   d. Hygiene factors

4. _____ refers to an individual's desire for significant accomplishment, mastering of skills, control, or high standards. The term was introduced by the psychologist, David McClelland.

   _____ is related to the difficulty of tasks people choose to undertake.

## Chapter 19. Motivation: Treat others as you would like to be treated

a. Need for power
b. Need for achievement
c. 1990 Clean Air Act
d. Two-factor theory


5. The _____ is a term that was popularised by David McClelland and describes a person's need to feel a sense of involvement and 'belonging' within a social group. However, it should be recognised that McClellend's thinking was strongly influenced by the pioneering work of Henry Murray who first identified underlying psychological human needs and motivational processes (1938.) It was Murray who set out a taxonomy of needs, including Achievement, Power and Affiliation - and placed these in the context of an integrated motivational model.

a. Strong-Campbell Interest Inventory
b. SESAMO
c. Polynomial conjoint measurement
d. Need for affiliation


6. _____ is a term that was popularized by renowned psychologist David McClelland in 1961. However, it should be recognized that McClellend's thinking was strongly influenced by the pioneering work of Henry Murray who first identified underlying psychological human needs and motivational processes (1938.) It was Murray who set out a taxonomy of needs, including Achievement, Power and Affiliation - and placed these in the context of an integrated motivational model.

a. 1990 Clean Air Act
b. Need for power
c. Need for Achievement
d. Two-factor theory


7. In law, _____ is the term to describe a partnership between two or more parties.

In England a number of statutes on the subject have been passed, the chief being the Bastardy Act of 1845, and the Bastardy Laws Amendment Acts of 1872 and 1873. The mother of a bastard may summon the putative father to petty sessions within twelve months of the birth (or at any later time if he is proved to have contributed to the child's support within twelve months after the birth), and the justices, as after hearing evidence on both sides, may, if the mother's evidence be corroborated in some material particular, adjudge the man to be the putative father of the child, and order him to pay a sum not exceeding five shillings a week for its maintenance, together with a sum for expenses incidental to the birth, or the funeral expenses, if it has died before the date of order, and the costs of the proceedings.

a. Affiliation
b. Affiliation
c. Adam Smith
d. Abraham Harold Maslow

8. _____ attempts to explain relational satisfaction in terms of perceptions of fair/unfair distributions of resources within interpersonal relationships. _____ is considered as one of the justice theories, It was first developed in 1962 by John Stacey Adams, a workplace and behavioral psychologist, who asserted that employees seek to maintain equity between the inputs that they bring to a job and the outcomes that they receive from it against the perceived inputs and outcomes of others (Adams, 1965.) The belief is that people value fair treatment which causes them to be motivated to keep the fairness maintained within the relationships of their co-workers and the organization.
   a. Equity theory
   b. A4e
   c. A Stake in the Outcome
   d. AAAI

9. _____ is about the mental processes regarding choice, or choosing. It explains the processes that an individual undergoes to make choices. In organizational behavior study, _____ is a motivation theory first proposed by Victor Vroom of the Yale School of Management.
   a. A Stake in the Outcome
   b. A4e
   c. AAAI
   d. Expectancy theory

10. _____ has become one of the most popular theories in organizational psychology.

Goal setting has been a formula used for acheivement since the early 1800s. The form and pattern has cahanged drastically over the years and there is still much debate as to what is the most efective pattern to follow.

   a. Human relations
   b. Job satisfaction
   c. Corporate Culture
   d. Goal-setting theory

## Chapter 19. Motivation: Treat others as you would like to be treated

11. _____ is the use of consequences to modify the occurrence and form of behavior. _____ is distinguished from classical conditioning (also called respondent conditioning, or Pavlovian conditioning) in that _____ deals with the modification of 'voluntary behavior' or operant behavior. Operant behavior 'operates' on the environment and is maintained by its consequences, while classical conditioning deals with the conditioning of respondent behaviors which are elicited by antecedent conditions.

   a. Occupational Safety and Health Administration
   b. Operant conditioning
   c. Unemployment insurance
   d. Outsourcing

12. In operant conditioning, _____ occurs when an event following a response causes an increase in the probability of that response occurring in the future. Response strength can be assessed by measures such as the frequency with which the response is made (for example, a pigeon may peck a key more times in the session), or the speed with which it is made (for example, a rat may run a maze faster.) The environment change contingent upon the response is called a reinforcer.

   a. Meetings, Incentives, Conferences, and Exhibitions
   b. Historiometry
   c. Diminishing Manufacturing Sources and Material Shortages
   d. Reinforcement

13. _____ refers to training in different ways to improve overall performance. It takes advantage of the particular effectiveness of each training method, while at the same time attempting to neglect the shortcomings of that method by combining it with other methods that address its weaknesses.

Cross training is employee-employer field means, training employees to do one another's work.

   a. Cross-training
   b. 1990 Clean Air Act
   c. 28-hour day
   d. 33 Strategies of War

## Chapter 20. Motivational Dynamics: Money isn't everything, the job counts too

1. _____ is a term describing performance-related pay, most frequently in the context of educational reform. It provides bonuses for workers who perform their jobs better, according to measurable criteria. In the United States, policy makers are divided on whether _____ should be offered to public school teachers, as is commonly the case in the United Kingdom.
   a. Real wage
   b. Performance-related pay
   c. Profit-sharing agreement
   d. Merit pay

2. _____, when used as a special term, refers to various incentive plans introduced by businesses that provide direct or indirect payments to employees that depend on company's profitability in addition to employees' regular salary and bonuses. In publicly traded companies these plans typically amount to allocation of shares to employees.

   The _____ plans are based on predetermined economic sharing rules that define the split of gains between the company as a principal and the employee as an agent.

   a. Profit sharing
   b. Federal Wage System
   c. Wage
   d. Living wage

3. In finance, an _____ is a contract between a buyer and a seller that gives the buyer the right--but not the obligation--to buy or to sell a particular asset (the underlying asset) at a later day at an agreed price. In return for granting the _____, the seller collects a payment (the premium) from the buyer. A call _____ gives the buyer the right to buy the underlying asset; a put _____ gives the buyer of the _____ the right to sell the underlying asset.
   a. A4e
   b. AAAI
   c. A Stake in the Outcome
   d. Option

4. _____ is the use of control systems (such as numerical control, programmable logic control, and other industrial control systems), in concert with other applications of information technology (such as computer-aided technologies [CAD, CAM, CAx]), to control industrial machinery and processes, reducing the need for human intervention. In the scope of industrialization, _____ is a step beyond mechanization. Whereas mechanization provided human operators with machinery to assist them with the physical requirements of work, _____ greatly reduces the need for human sensory and mental requirements as well.

## Chapter 20. Motivational Dynamics: Money isn't everything, the job counts too

a. Automation
b. A Stake in the Outcome
c. AAAI
d. A4e

5. In organizational development (OD), _____ is the application of Socio-Technical Systems principles and techniques to the humanization of work.

The aims of _____ to improved job satisfaction, to improved through-put, to improved quality and to reduced employee problems, e.g., grievances, absenteeism.

Under scientific management people would be directed by reason and the problems of industrial unrest would be appropriately (i.e., scientifically) addressed.

a. Work design
b. Path-goal theory
c. Graduate recruitment
d. Management process

6. _____ means increasing the scope of a job through extending the range of its job duties and responsibilities. This contradicts the principles of specialisation and the division of labour whereby work is divided into small units, each of which is performed repetitively by an individual worker. Some motivational theories suggest that the boredom and alienation caused by the division of labour can actually cause efficiency to fall.

a. Delayering
b. Mock interview
c. Job enlargement
d. Centralization

7. _____ is an approach to management development where an individual is moved through a schedule of assignments designed to give him or her a breadth of exposure to the entire operation.

_____ is also practiced to allow qualified employees to gain more insights into the processes of a company, and to reduce boredom and increase job satisfaction through job variation.

The term _____ can also mean the scheduled exchange of persons in offices, especially in public offices, prior to the end of incumbency or the legislative period.

a. 1990 Clean Air Act
b. 33 Strategies of War
c. 28-hour day
d. Job rotation


8. In mathematical logic, _____ is a valid argument and rule of inference which makes the inference that, if the conjunction A and B is true, then A is true, and B is true.

In formal language:

$$A \wedge B \vdash A$$

or

$$A \wedge B \vdash B$$

The argument has one premise, namely a conjunction, and one often uses _____ in longer arguments to derive one of the conjuncts.

An example in English:

It's raining and it's pouring.

a. 1990 Clean Air Act
b. Validity
c. Fuzzy logic
d. Simplification


9. _____ is an attempt to motivate employees by giving them the opportunity to use the range of their abilities. It is an idea that was developed by the American psychologist Frederick Herzberg in the 1950s. It can be contrasted to job enlargement which simply increases the number of tasks without changing the challenge.
a. Catfish effect
b. C-A-K-E
c. Job enrichment
d. Cash cow


10. In mathematics, a _____ law is (roughly speaking) a formal power series behaving as if it were the product of a Lie group. They were first defined in 1946 by S. Bochner. The term _____ sometimes means the same as _____ law, and sometimes means one of several generalizations.

## Chapter 20. Motivational Dynamics: Money isn't everything, the job counts too 87

   a. 28-hour day
   b. 1990 Clean Air Act
   c. 33 Strategies of War
   d. Formal group


11. _____, e-commuting, e-work, telework, working from home (WFH), or working at home (WAH) is a work arrangement in which employees enjoy flexibility in working location and hours. In other words, the daily commute to a central place of work is replaced by telecommunication links. Many work from home, while others, occasionally also referred to as nomad workers or web commuters utilize mobile telecommunications technology to work from coffee shops or myriad other locations.
   a. 33 Strategies of War
   b. Telecommuting
   c. 1990 Clean Air Act
   d. 28-hour day


12. The legal _____ varies from nation to nation. The weekend is a part of the week usually lasting one or two days in which most paid workers do not work.

In Muslim-majority countries the legal work week in the Middle East is typically either Saturday through Wednesday , Saturday through Thursday or Sunday through Thursday as in Egypt.

   a. Day One Christian Ministries
   b. Business day
   c. Workweek
   d. Working Time Directive

## Chapter 21. Teams and Teamwork: Two heads really can be better than one

1. A _____ is a group of employees from various functional areas of the organization - research, engineering, marketing, finance, human resources, and operations, for example - who are all focused on a specific objective and are responsible to work as a team to improve coordination and innovation across divisions and resolve mutual problems.
   a. Graduate recruitment
   b. Sociotechnical systems
   c. Cross-functional team
   d. Goal-setting theory

2. _____ refers to the movement of cash into or out of a business or financial product. It is usually measured during a specified, finite period of time. Measurement of _____ can be used

   - to determine a project's rate of return or value. The time of _____s into and out of projects are used as inputs in financial models such as internal rate of return, and net present value.
   - to determine problems with a business's liquidity. Being profitable does not necessarily mean being liquid. A company can fail because of a shortage of cash, even while profitable.
   - as an alternate measure of a business's profits when it is believed that accrual accounting concepts do not represent economic realities. For example, a company may be notionally profitable but generating little operational cash (as may be the case for a company that barters its products rather than selling for cash.) In such a case, the company may be deriving additional operating cash by issuing shares evaluating default risk, re-investment requirements, etc.

   _____ is a generic term used differently depending on the context. It may be defined by users for their own purposes.

   a. Sweat equity
   b. Gross profit margin
   c. Gross profit
   d. Cash flow

3. A _____ is a volunteer group composed of workers (or even students), usually under the leadership of their supervisor (but they can elect a team leader), who are trained to identify, analyse and solve work-related problems and present their solutions to management in order to improve the performance of the organization, and motivate and enrich the work of employees. When matured, true _____s become self-managing, having gained the confidence of management.
   _____s are an alternative to the dehumanising concept of the Division of Labour, where workers or individuals are treated like robots.
   a. Certified in Production and Inventory Management
   b. Competency-based job descriptions
   c. Connectionist expert systems
   d. Quality circle

## Chapter 21. Teams and Teamwork: Two heads really can be better than one

4. A _____ -- also known as a geographically dispersed team -- is a group of individuals who work across time, space, and organizational boundaries with links strengthened by webs of communication technology. They have complementary skills and are committed to a common purpose, have interdependent performance goals, and share an approach to work for which they hold themselves mutually accountable. Geographically dispersed teams allow organizations to hire and retain the best people regardless of location.
   a. Trademark
   b. Kanban
   c. Virtual team
   d. Risk management

5. In the social psychology of groups, _____ is the phenomenon of people making less effort to achieve a goal when they work in a group than when they work alone. This is seen as one of the main reasons groups are sometimes less productive than the combined performance of their members working as individuals.

   - Ringelmann, Max : 1913

   Research began in 1913 with Max Ringelmann's study. He found that when he asked a group of men to pull on a rope, that they did not pull as hard, or put as much effort into the activity, as they did when they were pulling alone.

   a. Machiavellianism
   b. Self-enhancement
   c. Personal space
   d. Social loafing

6. _____ is the term used to describe a situation where different entities cooperate advantageously for a final outcome. Simply defined, it means that the whole is greater than the sum of the individual parts. Although the whole will be greater than each individual part, this is not the concept of _____.
   a. 33 Strategies of War
   b. 1990 Clean Air Act
   c. 28-hour day
   d. Synergy

7. _____ is the study of groups, and also a general term for group processes. Relevant to the fields of psychology, sociology, and communication studies, a group is two or more individuals who are connected to each other by social relationships. Because they interact and influence each other, groups develop a number of dynamic processes that separate them from a random collection of individuals.

## Chapter 21. Teams and Teamwork: Two heads really can be better than one

a. Collective action
b. 1990 Clean Air Act
c. Group dynamics
d. 28-hour day

8. _____ has been described as the 'process of social influence in which one person can enlist the aid and support of others in the accomplishment of a common task'. A definition more inclusive of followers comes from Alan Keith of Genentech who said '_____ is ultimately about creating a way for people to contribute to making something extraordinary happen.'

_____ is one of the most salient aspects of the organizational context. However, defining _____ has been challenging.

a. 28-hour day
b. Leadership
c. Situational leadership
d. 1990 Clean Air Act

9. _____ is a type of thought exhibited by group members who try to minimize conflict and reach consensus without critically testing, analyzing, and evaluating ideas. Individual creativity, uniqueness, and independent thinking are lost in the pursuit of group cohesiveness, as are the advantages of reasonable balance in choice and thought that might normally be obtained by making decisions as a group. During _____, members of the group avoid promoting viewpoints outside the comfort zone of consensus thinking.

a. Self-report inventory
b. Diffusion of responsibility
c. Psychological statistics
d. Groupthink

## Chapter 22. Conflict and Negotiation: A smooth ride isn't always the best ride

1. _____ is a range of processes aimed at alleviating or eliminating sources of conflict. The term '_____' is sometimes used interchangeably with the term dispute resolution or alternative dispute resolution. Processes of _____ generally include negotiation, mediation and diplomacy.
   a. 28-hour day
   b. 1990 Clean Air Act
   c. Conflict resolution
   d. 33 Strategies of War

2. _____ is a recursive process where two or more people or organizations work together in an intersection of common goals -- for example, an intellectual endeavor that is creative in nature--by sharing knowledge, learning and building consensus. _____ does not require leadership and can sometimes bring better results through decentralization and egalitarianism. In particular, teams that work collaboratively can obtain greater resources, recognition and reward when facing competition for finite resources. _____ is also present in opposing goals exhibiting the notion of adversarial _____, though this is not a common case for using the term.
   a. 28-hour day
   b. 1990 Clean Air Act
   c. Collectivism
   d. Collaboration

3. _____, a form of alternative dispute resolution (ADR), is a legal technique for the resolution of disputes outside the courts, wherein the parties to a dispute refer it to one or more persons (the 'arbitrators', 'arbiters' or 'arbitral tribunal'), by whose decision (the 'award') they agree to be bound. It is a settlement technique in which a third party reviews the case and imposes a decision that is legally binding for both sides. Other forms of ADR include mediation (a form of settlement negotiation facilitated by a neutral third party) and non-binding resolution by experts.
   a. A4e
   b. AAAI
   c. A Stake in the Outcome
   d. Arbitration

4. _____, a form of alternative dispute resolution (ADR) or 'appropriate dispute resolution', aims to assist two (or more) disputants in reaching an agreement. The parties themselves determine the conditions of any settlements reached-- rather than accepting something imposed by a third party. The disputes may involve (as parties) states, organizations, communities, individuals or other representatives with a vested interest in the outcome.
   a. Meritor Savings Bank v. Vinson
   b. Mediation
   c. Foreign Corrupt Practices Act
   d. Maximum medical improvement

## Chapter 23. Innovation and Change: Change can be your best friend

1. _____ is, in very basic words, a position a firm occupies against its competitors.

According to Michael Porter, the three methods for creating a sustainable _____ are through:

1. Cost leadership

2. Differentiation

3. Focus (economics)

   a. Competitive advantage
   b. 28-hour day
   c. 1990 Clean Air Act
   d. Theory Z


2. The process of _____ involves the introduction of a good or service that is new or substantially improved. This includes, but is not limited to, improvements in functional characteristics, technical abilities, or ease of use.
   a. Service-profit chain
   b. Letter of resignation
   c. Job enlargement
   d. Product innovation


3. _____ is a form of social influence. It is the process of guiding people and oneself toward the adoption of an idea, attitude, or action by rational and symbolic (though not always logical) means. It is strategy of problem-solving relying on 'appeals' rather than coercion.
   a. Self-enhancement
   b. Persuasion
   c. Personal space
   d. Social loafing


4. _____. The objective of OD is to improve the organization's capacity to handle its internal and external functioning and relationships. This would include such things as improved interpersonal and group processes, more effective communication, enhanced ability to cope with organizational problems of all kinds, more effective decision processes, more appropriate leadership style, improved skill in dealing with destructive conflict, and higher levels of trust and cooperation among organizational members.
   a. Organizational structure
   b. Organizational development
   c. Improved Organizational Performance
   d. Industrial relations

# ANSWER KEY

### Chapter 1
1. a  2. a  3. d  4. c  5. d  6. d  7. d  8. d  9. a  10. b
11. d  12. d  13. d  14. d  15. d  16. d  17. d

### Chapter 2
1. d  2. d  3. d  4. c  5. d  6. d  7. c  8. d  9. a  10. d
11. d

### Chapter 3
1. a  2. b  3. d  4. c  5. a  6. b  7. d  8. b  9. a  10. a
11. d  12. a  13. a

### Chapter 4
1. d  2. a  3. c  4. a  5. a  6. c  7. a  8. b  9. d  10. d
11. b  12. d

### Chapter 5
1. a  2. a  3. d  4. d  5. d  6. b

### Chapter 6
1. d  2. b  3. a  4. a  5. d  6. a  7. d  8. c

### Chapter 7
1. b  2. c  3. b  4. d  5. a  6. b  7. a  8. d  9. d  10. c
11. d  12. b  13. d  14. d  15. d  16. c

### Chapter 8
1. d  2. d  3. d  4. a  5. d  6. d  7. d  8. c  9. b  10. b
11. d  12. d  13. a  14. b  15. c

### Chapter 9
1. d  2. c  3. d  4. d  5. d  6. a  7. d  8. d  9. a  10. d
11. c

### Chapter 10
1. b  2. a  3. d  4. d  5. a  6. c  7. d  8. b  9. a  10. d
11. d

### Chapter 11
1. a  2. d  3. d  4. d  5. d  6. d  7. d  8. c  9. d  10. b
11. d  12. d  13. c  14. d  15. b  16. d  17. a  18. d

### Chapter 12
1. d  2. d  3. d  4. d  5. a  6. b  7. a  8. d  9. b  10. c
11. d  12. b  13. d  14. b  15. d  16. d

## Chapter 13
1. d    2. b    3. d    4. a    5. d    6. d    7. c    8. a

## Chapter 14
1. d    2. b    3. c    4. a    5. d    6. a    7. d

## Chapter 15
1. d    2. a    3. d    4. d    5. d    6. d    7. d    8. b    9. d    10. d
11. d    12. d    13. d    14. b    15. c    16. c    17. a    18. b    19. b    20. b
21. a    22. d    23. a    24. b    25. d    26. d    27. d    28. b    29. d    30. c
31. d

## Chapter 16
1. d    2. b    3. d    4. c    5. c    6. d    7. d    8. c    9. b    10. c

## Chapter 17
1. d    2. a    3. d

## Chapter 18
1. a    2. d    3. d    4. a    5. a    6. b    7. a    8. b    9. b    10. b
11. a    12. b    13. d    14. c

## Chapter 19
1. a    2. c    3. d    4. b    5. d    6. b    7. b    8. a    9. d    10. d
11. b    12. d    13. a

## Chapter 20
1. d    2. a    3. d    4. a    5. a    6. c    7. d    8. d    9. c    10. d
11. b    12. c

## Chapter 21
1. c    2. d    3. d    4. c    5. d    6. d    7. c    8. b    9. d

## Chapter 22
1. c    2. d    3. d    4. b

## Chapter 23
1. a    2. d    3. b    4. c

www.ingramcontent.com/pod-product-compliance
Lightning Source LLC
Chambersburg PA
CBHW081846230426
43669CB00018B/2839